Thai Girl Naked: A Former Bangkok Bargirl Tells All

Noi Thawattana

Published by Noi Thawattana, 2025.

While every precaution has been taken in the preparation of this book, the publisher assumes no responsibility for errors or omissions, or for damages resulting from the use of the information contained herein.

THAI GIRL NAKED: A FORMER BANGKOK BARGIRL TELLS ALL

First edition. November 20, 2025.

Copyright © 2025 Noi Thawattana.

ISBN: 978-1512086522

Written by Noi Thawattana.

Also by Noi Thawattana

We're Not Supposed to Tell You: Sex Slavery, Drugs, and Other
Secrets of Thailand's Prostitution Industry
Thai Girl Naked: A Former Bangkok Bargirl Tells All

Table of Contents

The Smile Economy

My name is Noi, and I worked as a "special massage" girl, a "hostess club" girl, and yes, as a "Soi Cowboy" girl. I did have sex for money, although most of that my sex-industry life consisted of more gray-area transactions, not direct sex for money. You know that Thai culture has a lot of gray areas, right? Consider the entire sex industry in Thailand. If you read the Thai law code, prostitution is strictly illegal, and anyone engaging in any form of prostitution is to be hauled off to prison for a long time! And in many other facets of everyday life, we don't quite follow black-and-white what is prescribed in books, including in the way we practice Buddhism.

That should make it more interesting for you to read this book, because you can't learn about Thailand if you only read the official books. An official law book might tell you one thing, and someone on the street might tell you exactly the opposite thing, and where is the truth? Well the thing closest to the truth is probably something only Thai people usually know, only because we have lived in Thailand and speak the language, but it's not difficult or incomprehensible for foreigners. If you picked up this book, it already means you're brave and curious enough to have asked. So I'm going to answer.

In this book I'm going to tell you the real truth about being a Thai girl, being a bargirl, and even being a hostess and massage girl, which I've done too. I'll also tell you about being a Thai girl moving to America on a fiancée visa, because that's something I also did. I'm going to be honest, because there's no reason for me not to be honest. I'm writing a book and putting it out to an audience that mostly doesn't know me, so I don't mind what you think of me. Your Thai girlfriend or another Thai girl you meet? Well, she cares a *lot* about what you think of her, so she might not be perfectly honest with you. As you might already know, "honesty" is a pretty loosely defined term in Thailand. It basically means not veering too far away from the truth, while maintaining social harmony and obedience to the social hierarchy. I don't claim to have completely broken away from that Thai thinking. But I am asserting to you here that by writing a book and sending it out, in English, to the big wide world, I feel free to say many things that I or other Thai girls would never say in person.

I've had a lot of things on the tip of my tongue (good English expression, right?) for a long time. I often wanted to tell foreign men I met about the truths of bargirls or just Thai girls in general or our lives, but telling them the truth at that moment would have meant hurting my relationship with them, hurting my income from them, and maybe hurting my friends' and coworkers' incomes with them. Hurting relationships just to tell someone the "absolute truth," would be a very un-Thai thing to do, even for a slightly non-typical Thai girl like me.

I finished high school in Bangkok before I started working in the "love business," and here in the United States, I am now attending college, with a major in English and Creative Writing. That doesn't make me better than the average Bangkok prostitute or ex-prostitute, but it makes me a lot more capable of writing my thoughts into an English-language book, and also, having a little bit of education and living now in America lets me have a little bit of distance from my origins and past work, so I can think about them more objectively.

Even though I'm now in America and I love it, this book isn't a sob story about how terrible it was to be born in Thailand in modest financial means. My life is good. Even when I was a bargirl, my life wasn't so terrible. Anyway, is anyone's life perfect? I don't think so. I think I'm happier than the average person. So the goal of this book isn't getting pity from you. I not only don't want your pity, but I don't deserve it. Here I am, living in a first-world country, drinking a Starbucks drink, sitting in front of a Macbook, writing a *book*! That's a pretty good life already.

The Identity Illusion

This book is called *Thai Girl Naked,* not just *Naked Girl.* So it's going to talk specifically about a Thai girl's life and attitude and experience. But what exactly is a Thai girl? What makes us Thai? That's not a question that's only for the philosophers. It's actually a really important question, even now in Thai politics when central Thais are calling the northeastern Thais "not real Thais," and all sides in general are accusing one another of not being Thai enough. Actually those kinds of doubts are seldom voiced in Thai culture. We are usually taught that Thai-ness is a completely clear-cut black-and-white thing, and once a Thai always a Thai, and it's obvious who is Thai, and so on. Going to school in Thailand, one of the things we constantly hear is that "the Thai people are one," and that there's a defining force of Thai unity across regions and social classes and ethnicities and so on. Of course, we're told that the King is the personification of that unity, but (and this becomes more important practically in Thailand as the King becomes old and frail and, like any human being, the King will eventually die), that Thai unity and Thai-ness are greater even than the person of the King, and have defined Thailand since all time and far into the future.

When I started improving my English and preparing to move to America, and especially once I moved to America, I started reading and researching more about Thai-ness. I wanted to know more about myself as a Thai person, so I could become certain of exactly what made me Thai when I went to a foreign place. As would be the case for any young person trying to discover truth beyond what they learned in elementary school, the truth was a lot more complicated than the fairytale we were taught in school. I read books and websites that questioned a lot of the basic tenets of what I thought being Thai was about. And even before reading those things, I already knew that rich and poor in Thailand have serious conflict, and it's not always "all Thais stand together," although I also knew that in the Thai conception of things, the rich ruling the poor was in fact the form of "standing together." Standing together in formation, strong over weak, like an ancient Thai Buddhist statue. But anyway, this isn't a book about analyzing Thai history, but about Thai girls. So the more important thing for you to learn here is not that Thai history is more complicated than the simple school version, but that what regular Thai girls believe and know about Thai history is a very, very simple version.

My childish ideas of black-and-white Thai-ness were actually first challenged when I was Japanese. Wait, when I was Japanese? Well, like many things you find at night in Thailand, I wasn't exactly the authentic product. But the customers didn't know. As far as they could tell, I was perfectly Japanese. Just like those wallets they sell at Thai street markets are perfectly Gucci! I worked in a "kapoo club." "Kapoo" is a pun in Thai on the words for penis and testicles. So it's something like a "cock and balls club." And the idea of a "kapoo" club is providing only handjobs, from pretty girls who are supposedly "not professional prostitutes."

In reality, both parts of that story are completely false. Almost every girl in every kapoo shop will provide full sex. But she'll tell the customer that she's doing that only for him because he's so special and handsome, to make him feel unique and as if he's getting something special just from her (and also to prevent him from trying other girls at the shop). You see how the trick works? And also, the girls in a kapoo shop are generally from the same backgrounds as any other Thai prostitutes. They are not any more likely to be university students or upper-class girls (ha ha) than the girls at any other prostitution venue in Bangkok. I guess there are fewer Isaan girls, just because kapoo shops are aimed at Thai men, who don't like dark skin, but there are still lots of light-skinned Issan girls in the kapoo scene.

Some kapoo shops provide girls who are supposed to be "hiso" (high society, from rich families). Some kapoo shops provide girls who are supposed to be "university students." And the one I worked in provided girls who were supposed to be "Japanese." We were of course just about as Japanese as those other girls were "high society" or "university students." Meaning we weren't Japanese at all. But the point is, with the proper makeup and training, I don't know of any customers who actually had any idea that we weren't really Japanese.

Every "Kapoo" girl laughs at the whole premise, and knows full well that in reality she's as much a prostitute as every other prostitute, and of course she knows she's not really a Japanese girl or a university student or a rich hiso (society) girl, but what's important here is not the girls' self-esteem, but the customers' perceptions! The girls know they're prostitutes, but the customers believe they aren't. And you can imagine: the customers get turned on by the idea of a pretty girl who is not, not, not a hooker handling their most intimate parts and giving them a sumptuous orgasm with their slippery hands. The "not a hooker" illusion is done all across the Thai sex industry, but we'll talk about that later. For now, let's stick to kapoo clubs. Cock and balls shops.

There are all sorts of kapoo clubs, around various fantasy themes. And as far as I know, they are only for a Thai or Thai-speaking audience, so if you are a foreigner in Thailand, you may never have heard of "kapoo" even if you are an expert on paid sex shops. Oh, but this is my lesson on how elusive "Thai-ness" is, so maybe I shouldn't say that so firmly yet.

And, as I said, the one I worked in was supposed to provide Japanese girls. It was called (don't laugh... or laugh, I don't care) Harajuku Girls, and it was hidden away in an office building. And we, the girls who worked there, were supposed to pretend to be Japanese. Now, let me note here. Of course we were all Thai girls. But as far as the customer was concerned, this was not a shop where Thai girls pretended to be Japanese. This wasn't like going to see a movie and enjoying it even though you know it's not real. As far as the customer was concerned, we were real, genuine Japanese girls. According to the story told our customers, we were Japanese girls who were the daughters of Japanese businessmen in Thailand, and we worked at this kapoo shop to supplement our pocket money.

So here we were, Thai girls pretending to be Japanese, Harajuku Girls, and with Thai guys fully believing that we were Japanese. Oh, but weren't we told in school that Thai people are definitely Thai and so different from any other race that they would instantly recognize each other from ten kilometers' distance? It just wasn't so.

And it was not only comical to me, but also educational, to see how with some funny accents and different clothes and of course dyed hair, we could be fully convincingly Japanese, even to Thai men. Besides being layered in makeup and dressed in our mamasan's best idea of what Harajuku girls dress like (bell bottom jeans! platform shoes! fur-lined hoodie jackets!), we were instructed to never, ever speak Thai, other than an intentionally "Japanese accented" sawadeeka! In fact, we were taught basic Japanese to mumble to the customers to improve the illusion. The scariest part was that some of the Thai customers actually did speak Japanese, but we made a good show of not understanding much of what they were saying, supposedly because their Japanese wasn't good enough for our native Japanese ears to understand, but of course really because none of us spoke any significant amount of Japanese.

There were some slip ups of course. They probably damaged our shop's reputation, and I don't know whether the customers went to tell their friends that his girl was not really Japanese, or whether they continued to suspend disbelief and took their moment of revelation in solitary shame.

The slip ups always happened exactly the same way. Always either in the middle of the sex act, or at the end when finishing up. When the girl was either busy screaming and acting like she was having a billion orgasms, and forgot to also act like she's a *Japanese* girl having a billion orgasms—or when the entertainment session was winding down and the girl was starting to let her guard down.

I am not a doctor or a psychologist but I think people only have a certain strength or capacity for lying or acting, and when you exceed their capacity, there's going to be a breakdown. It's like when your web browser crashes when you open too many windows. There were always a few funny stories about in the heat of the action, a girl yelling "faster" or "slower" or "that hurts" in Thai, and getting a customer to seriously doubt her Japanese-ness. It was up to the girl whether she could rescue the situation and say that she can speak a little bit of Thai. Of course every time that happened, mamasan would give us more lessons about how to act Japanese even in such moments, and the proper Japanese expressions to say, but who can remember all that, especially when we're also trying to remember how to sexually please a man to make him return next time and give us a big tip this time?

Love as Survival

"Thai girls only want money." Or, "My Thai girlfriend only sees me as an ATM." Or, "Thai girls only care about my financial status."

There's a lot of truth to that! But also a lot of misunderstanding.

In Thai culture, as in many Asian cultures, marriage is primarily about the harsh realities of physical and material survival, not about romance and flowers. The idea of "romantic" marriage is still very new in Thailand, and even the richer and more educated classes only partially believe in it. For most people in Thailand, and certainly for less educated and more traditional Thai people, marriage is all about securing or improving your family's access to food, housing, cellphones, and pickup trucks. And it's straightforwardly so. I know it would be unusual in America to find a single woman who, when she is asked what kind of guy she's looking for, would openly say "most important is that he's rich and provides for me." Even if an American woman *thinks* it, she'd never openly *say* it. Well, we Thais are beat-around-the-bush people in some regards, but in terms of the purpose of marriage being practical and material, we are very straightforward! A Thai woman will tell you directly that she's looking for a well-off man, and even that you don't have enough money to be satisfactory for her.

Or at least that's what she would do in Thai culture. But most of the Thai women that foreigners meet have been accustomed to Western standards, where it's considered rude to openly say that she's looking for a man who will give her money. Such a woman, say a woman working in the foreigner tourist industry and dating white European or American or Australian foreigners, still wants and expects that financial support. But she conforms to the Western standard only in what she says: she *claims* she only wants a man who makes her heart flutter and who's romantic or something. And that's where there's a disconnect. Her intentions and her culture and her real needs are in the traditional Thai mode of wanting marriage to financially support her. But she conforms to the Western standard, in the Thai standard of saying whatever it takes to smooth out a social situation, of claiming that she doesn't care about money. Yes, it's a Thai standard to say whatever is necessary, and in this case, she follows the Thai standard by claiming to follow the Western standard of not caring about money. I know it's confusing, but I think you know what I mean!

So now we might get some mixed expectations, when John from America meets Lek from Issan. And Lek has told him all along that she doesn't care about money and only about romance, even though that's completely against her cultural upbringing, and against any kind of evaluation of her needs in life (she's probably desperately poor, not desperately lonely). And then John gets upset when Lek often asks him for money!

I have two points with which I can defend Lek. First, of course, you can't singlehandedly change thousands of years of Thai history and traditions about marriage, nor can you change the economic realities of her life and of her family's needs and expectations, with a few words about love and romance. But the second thing is, wait, how did they usually meet? In what setting? In the setting of John paying Lek for sex! I mean that was probably their first conversation: John offering Lek some money to go home with him for the night. So it's just funny that John would act outraged when after they marry, she still expects money from him. Not only was she taking money from John for having sex, but her entire career was taking money from men in return for sex! Why is it surprising that she'd continue to want money for sex?

And when they got married, wasn't there a big deal about the sinsod, the traditional Thai dowry given by the groom to the parents, that should have given John some idea that Thai marriage is about the husband financially supporting the wife and her family! Wouldn't John see these clues? Would Lek act outraged if after they marry, he still expects sex from her? It kind of doesn't make sense to me.

I know. Westerners were brought up to believe that marriage is about pure emotion and companionship and family, completely apart from money and material things. But guess what: in the Western European first world, marriage was also primarily about money and survival, a few hundred years ago. As I learned in my *Tess of the D'Urbervilles* English literature class, the idea of marriage coming from romantic love only came about in Europe around the 18th century. That's not a very long time. Maybe because people who are generally struggling to survive, as most Europeans were in the past and most Thai people are now, are more concerned with making ends meet than with romantic or emotional notions of marriage? Or maybe because in the past, European culture was as focused on family survival, and not on individual fulfillment, as Thai culture is today? I don't know. I'm only an amateur student, not a professional historian or anthropologist. I just have some ideas about these things. But I think my point is don't vilify a Thai girl, especially a current or former bargirl, who expects financial support from her husband. It's in thousands of years of culture, it's in the social expectations, and it's exactly how it used to be in the Western world until pretty recently.

On the other hand, I do understand the usual foreign guy's point. Culture or no culture, he still feels terrible. "It's culture" or "Europe used to be the same" doesn't help the feelings of a man who's given everything to his wife and she still demands more. And so, my advice to men is not to hope to completely escape from the paradigm of "the man has to financially support the woman." You just can't hope for it. *Especially* if you're a foreign man meeting women in Thailand, because the women you are most likely to encounter are women seeking the most financial support—because foreigners are seen as being the most capable of providing financial support, especially for women who are not considered attractive by Thai men.

What I do recommend is at least trying to moderate her expectations and needs a bit. You can't do this long after you meet her. You can't fundamentally change a person. Just like you can't turn a dog into a cat. But when you're shopping for a pet, you can make sure whether you're getting a dog or a cat! And what I mean by that is you should carefully think about and even investigate your Thai girlfriend's financial situation before you get too serious with her. Is her whole family nonstop financial drama and crisis and always somebody is sick and needs 100,000 baht and has mafia debts and is going to lose their home and stuff like that? This kind of girlfriend can be fine for a short while, but she will be a never ending black hole of financial needs. Trust me, even after you have paid all her relatives' debts and mortgages and gambling losses, she will bring in a new set of relatives with a new set of problems. People like this just don't change. A better option is a girl (and now it's time for me to go *cough cough, like me!*) who has limited and finite financial needs, and who, along with her family, accepts some responsibility for her own financial situation.

I'm a Thai girl, so yes, I do expect my boyfriends to help me financially. Some could, some couldn't, but for those that couldn't, it definitely counted against them. But my needs were not never-ending and my family is not a (I love this American word) basketcase! For example, when our family-owned restaurant had a fire was one of the few times I asked a boyfriend for money—for 50,000 baht (about $1,500) for repairs to the restaurant—and noted that my family was exhausting all our savings paying for medical bills and other repairs from the fire. At that time, I was young, and my boyfriend (yes, a Thai boyfriend from my neighborhood, if you're keeping score) wasn't able to meet my request for money. And yes, I counted it against him. But I didn't dump him and didn't threaten to kill myself. I only knew that he was not the greatest long-term boyfriend for me if he could not provide me with any financial assistance. But note, that is the only time I asked him for money (other than accepting occasional gifts from him), and I made the request when telling him that my family would be paying most of the bills related to the fire, and not telling him that he, as the daughter's boyfriend, would have to pay all the bills. Do you see the difference?

I see foreigners in Thailand putting a lot of thought into which English school they teach in (yes, that's the usual job of foreigners in Thailand, even those foreigners who can't speak English well), which apartment they live in, and even which bar they drink in. But they really don't seem to put a lot of thought into which Thai girl they let deeply into their lives. Maybe that's just part of the "romantic love, not practical love" part of Western culture. But it's just so strange to me, in that I think Westerners are generally very thoughtful, logical, methodical people, but on this one point, choosing a Thai girl to let into their lives, they seem to forget all their logic and all their caution! They go based on first impressions and gut feelings and other things that are nice in romance stories, but as we Thai people know and advise, are not so good for long-term relationships or marriages.

So my advice to you is that you try to be more *Thai* in how you evaluate your mate. And despite what many farangs think, we Thai people are not stupid. We like to joke around, but we are also good at evaluating people, and evaluating a good long-term partner. (Although the Thai people the usual farang would encounter, especially in the sex industry, would often be exactly the ones who made the wrong decisions in evaluations in life.)

Try to remember with clear eyes how you met your Thai girlfriend. Even if she wasn't a prostitute, did you meet her in a place where her job is sweet-talking generous men? (For example, a massage shop or a hostess bar, both of which I've worked in.) Or did you make her interested in you by buying her a big present or giving her a big tip or telling her how well-off you are? In that case, you're really kind of asking for her trying to take more and more from you, because you found her when she was looking for guys who would provide many material things to her. In fact, in your imagination, take the whole thing back to your country, say America. If you met a stripper and she invited you on a date after you gave her a really big tip—you wouldn't be surprised if she kept asking you for money, would you? Well people are people everywhere in the world. You shouldn't expect a girl dancing nude for money to not want more money from you just because she's Thai and not American.

There are obligations to be sure if you are going to date or marry any Thai woman. Even a rich Thai woman expects financial support from her husband. Any Thai girl who tells you she will never, ever want a single baht from you is putting on an act. That's just not realistic, and such "I will never want any money from you" girls often turn out to be the neediest and most manipulative ones. I could tell you the stories that bring me to this conclusion, but trust me, because I know Thai girls (and I am one).

So if I've told you that nonstop drama is a bad sign, and "I will never want any money from you" is a bad sign, what's a good sign? What kind of Thai girl would I recommend for you to date and marry? I would say: choose one who acknowledges that you are expected to provide financial support to her and her family, but who puts that in very clear terms, with limits. In other words, a woman who sees you as a financial partner with a certain role to fulfill, and yes, a certain amount of money to provide, but not one who sees you as an inexhaustible source of more and more money for her family's every whim.

The kind-of-bad news is that many girls who have dated foreigners, or who know girls who have dated or married foreigners, have already adopted the mentality of "a foreign man will give you whatever amount of money you want, as long as you make a face, and maybe threaten to kill yourself." It's true, because many foreign men want to be good, or they are insecure and they want to be accepted, or because they don't know what is acceptable in Thai culture. Hey, take it from Thai men. Giving your girlfriend money is normal and accepted. But constantly giving her unlimited sums of money is definitely not normal and not accepted. This is true for Thai men in any social class and in any region of Thailand. And if you've wondered, yes, Thai men do laugh at foreign men behind their backs, that those fools just give girls anything they ask for (usually snidely adding that those are ugly girls in the first place!).

So, "when in Rome, do as the Romans." Which doesn't mean that when you come to Thailand, you should do as every other farang looking for a girlfriend in Thailand. What it means is when you come to Thailand, you should emulate Thai men. Thoroughly investigate any girl that is going to be more than a fling (a fling is called a "gik" in Thai, and of course any kind of girl is acceptable to a Thai man for a "gik," but the standards for a relationship are much higher). And don't expect to get into a relationship with a Thai woman without contributing any money. That's just a pipe dream, and any Thai man would tell you that it's not realistic. But make sure that the girl is reasonable, has limits, and doesn't go beyond those reasonable limits.

And actually, I think this is something Westerners already know, but somehow they forget it when they arrive in Thailand. Imagine if you married a woman in your own country, say Canada. Imagine she's a white, Canadian woman you met when she was, say, a waitress. If she came to you and said, "Honey, I need $500 every month for gas and Starbucks and clothes and whatnot," you'd probably consider it pretty reasonable. But imagine if she came to you every day or every week with a mountain of drama and crises and emergencies and always claimed that the world was going to blow up if you don't give her $1,000 immediately—bad choice in woman, right? You guys *already know this* for dating or marrying women back in your own countries, but somehow you forget it as soon as you arrive in Thailand!

Well, who knows. Maybe Thai guys are the same way. I've heard some stories about rich Thai guys getting cheated for money by women in the US, letting white American women (who are to them of course "exotic" and maybe "pure") do things they'd never let Thai women do to them. So we're all blind when we're out of our environments. Just try not to be too blind, especially when all a Thai girl wants from you is your money.

Handiwork

My story is typical in the way that everyone's story is typical. A little bit different, but with the same threads: family needs money, limited job opportunities, opportunity for fast money and meeting rich guys. Those are probably the same reasons girls got into the sex industry 4,000 years ago in ancient China or 200 years ago in Victorian England or today in New York City. (Oh, some Thai people will say that prostitution is only a Western invention, and brought to Thailand only by Westerners—please give us Thai people more credit! If what they said was true, Thai culture would be the only culture in the world that didn't have prostitution!)

My family ran a small restaurant, really more like a cafeteria, on the outskirts of Bangkok, in Pinklao. The whole family worked in the restaurant. My father was the boss of the whole enterprise, but he also served as the main cook. My mother alternated between cooking and taking payments. My sister and a few cousins and one aunt all helped out too, cooking, cleaning, carrying trays, and all the usual restaurant functions. All together, the restaurant usually made about 50,000 baht (about $1,800 USD) per month, but that's before paying anyone's salary. We had to pay out that 50,000 baht to all the relatives helping out, and usually what was left for my parents and my sister and me was about 20,000 baht a month. That's still not a bad income in Thailand, especially since we owned our own house (we lived above the restaurant, and the whole house was inherited by my father from my great aunt), so we didn't have to worry about paying monthly rent, and we rented out the restaurant premises as sleeping quarters at night (after the restaurant closed) to an Issan family for a little more income.

We were doing ok. In fact, when I talked with some of the Isaan girls in the Soi Cowboy scene, I realized my family had been doing *very* ok, when compared with how little their families had had. And unlike the case with their families, my family didn't have any "mama drama" or anything like that. My parents didn't have any violent fights or heavy drinking or criminal relatives or anything like that. It was a pretty ok average Bangkok life.

I graduated from high school (called "mathayom" in Thai), and was considering becoming a shop clerk or an office lady. I didn't have that much interest in going to university at the time, and I was eager to start earning an income, although I did intend to study maybe accounting or IT while I worked.

Meanwhile, we were having problems at the family restaurant. My aunt had quit, for a much higher paying job being a waitress in an upscale restaurant. When we tried to talk to candidates to replace her, family or not, they wanted to be paid much more than we could afford. A new MK (Thai hotpot restaurant, kind of the Denny's or Applebee's of Thailand) opened just down the road from our restaurant's location, and business was down. And, as if working in sequence, fire broke out in the kitchen of our restaurant, and seriously damaged the restaurant area (although not our rooms upstairs). My father was injured in the fire, and had a hospital bill of about 30,000 baht, which used a big part of our savings.

Foreigners always have an idea that Thai people are so kind and generous and open-hearted and all the other things. I really think that's because the only Thai people they meet are much poorer than they are, and are generally serving them in hotels or in the sex industry. Those Thai people smile and are nice because it's their job to smile and be nice. Sure, Thai people are nice to family and friends, just like any humans anywhere in the world would be. And Thai people know how to be "nice" (more accurately, to give face or respect) when it's necessary in the Thai social hierarchy.

But when foreigners tell me "but Thai people are so nice; why didn't anyone just help your family after your restaurant burned down?" I have to give them an uncomfortable smile. Because no one in Thailand would help a stranger, unless that stranger was of higher status and somehow could give them merit or standing or rewards in the future. No one. Have you ever seen what happens in a Thai traffic accident? Bystanders quickly walk away from the scene, because they don't want to be involved or blamed. I was actually shocked the first time I saw a bicycle-car traffic accident happen on Newbury Street in Boston, and everyone was running toward the bicyclist lying on the ground; I thought they were going to loot his wallet or something! In Thailand, people don't help strangers, unless it's mandated by the hierarchy. So when you're a tourist, people will help you, because you're higher and richer in the hierarchy. But when you're a lower-middle-class family whose restaurant burned down, no one really wants to help you.

No one, not even my closest friends, offered me or my family any money to help. I had some part-time boyfriends and guy friends, but none of them were really in a financial situation where they could help me much. They were also struggling with money, and because they are boys, their families put a lot of demands on them to contribute money to the families, not to their girlfriends.

But I did have one high school friend who did me a big favor. She didn't give me any money. But she gave me a confession. She had mentioned that she is a secretary in an office somewhere in Thonburi (on the outskirts of Bangkok, across the river from the main city). I never questioned her about that. But when I had money problems, she confessed to me that she doesn't actually work in an office, but actually in a massage shop. She told me she earns about 40,000 baht per month. This is a great salary in Thailand even now for a college graduate, but we were only barely high school graduates, and this was about ten years ago, when salaries were much lower. So while she only called it a massage shop, when she told me what the salary is, I understood that it's a "special" massage shop (no one doing no-sex massage would earn that much), and I also understood why she had kept it all a secret from me.

She told me that it's not a bad way to make money. You don't have to have sex with the customers, only give them handjobs, which isn't so terrible. Just call it "kapoo" (penis and balls, also the name of the type of shop) massage. I didn't know at the time that you also offer full sex, or at least oral sex, to customers in order to improve your income and make the customer feel that he's having something special. But anyway, her suggestion was good. And the shop where she worked was too far from my family's home for me to commute to, but the same businesswoman owned another shop, Harajuku Girls, not as far from my home, where they were now hiring. At Harajuku Girls the girls were supposed to be "Japanese," and they were looking for girls who could pass for "Japanese." And I am light skinned enough so it wouldn't be a problem to pretend to be Japanese, and I guessed that I had watched enough Japanese movies and TV shows to know a little bit of the manners and the language!

And that's how I got to the point of working in the "body trade." So now you see that while the specifics of my story—being born in Bangkok, having graduated from high school—are different from the average bargirl story of having been born in rural poverty, the general end result at the crucial decision point is the same: my family needed money, and my job prospects were not that great. With a high school (mathayom) education and no experience other than working in the restaurant, it would be difficult to get any kind of office job. I would most likely end up working long hours as a shop seller or a restaurant hostess, for about 12,000 or 15,000 baht per month, which is where most of my friends had gone.

Despite tourists seeing many prostitutes in Bangkok, still, being a prostitute is not considered a normal thing in Thai society. My parents are not socialites; they are pretty simple lower middle class Bangkok working people. Yet they would not under any circumstances agree to me working in any kind of sex shop (can only theorize, because I've never told them). It's not that they think anything materially bad would happen to me. They wouldn't think I'd be in serious physical danger. But it's that they know that their Buddhist karma would be very damaged by their daughter doing something so un-Buddhist as having sex for money, and, in a more immediate way, their standing with their social group, our extended relatives and their friends and neighbors, would be definitely seriously tarnished if they associated with their daughter the "chicken." ("Chicken" is Thai slang for a prostitute, so be careful calling any Thai person a "chicken" if you mean it in the American way of someone who is scared, because in Thai it has only one meaning: a prostitute.).

You may have heard the stories about Issan (northeastern Thai rural area, where most Thai bargirls come from) people being very proud that their daughter is a bargirl and meets many foreigners, right? I still don't think that those parents are really proud that their daughter is a prostitute. If you actually talk to the proud parents of the Issan bargirl, they believe, or claim to believe, that their daughter is a waitress or a bartender or a cleaner or even a singer or a dancer, but that there's no prostitution involved. In many cases, the mother herself, or her close friends or relatives, have worked in the sex trade, so at some level they know what's going on. But in Thai culture, if we deny what's going on, then it's not going on. Even if the mother worked as a prostitute, having sex with men every night for money, she is willing to believe that her daughter working in the same bar now is a waitress and is meeting all these generous foreign men by only being a waitress.

And the point is here, even though tourists in Thailand see many prostitutes, you shouldn't think that prostitutes are a normal part of Thai society. They (we?) are definitely looked down upon. And one reason that many Thai prostitutes say that foreign men are better than Thai men is that no Thai man who has good dating prospects would ever date a prostitute. The only Thai men who are available for dating for bargirls are maybe small time thugs and thieves, or very rural, very poor (money is important for Thai dating!) guys. It's only natural that they'd think middle-class foreign guys are so rich and great. Actually, you can probably see much the same if you think about your own country. What kind of guy in your country would date or marry a prostitute? Probably not the most desirable guy (*Pretty Woman* is just a movie!). Well, Thai society is much more status conscious and exclusionary than your society, so imagine the exclusion toward prostitutes in your culture, and multiply it by a thousand to think about the attitude toward prostitutes from Thai people in Bangkok! Exaggerating? Not really.

So with my parents, I wouldn't dare risk them even thinking anything remotely related to prostitution about me. At the same time, I had to think of a good cover story, that would account for my being out in the evenings, and bringing home good money to help my parents. Without them thinking the obvious. And without them feeling inclined to check up on me. So the story I made up was that I am using my experience working in the family restaurant to work as a waitress in a private restaurant for foreign VIPs visiting some Thai company. And that because I speak decent English (and I did, because of high school in Bangkok and watching Hollywood movies), I was making good money in this restaurant, but also, this restaurant is an invitation-only private-venue thing just for the VIP foreigner clients of the company, no, my parents could not visit me at work or have dinner at the restaurant where I work, and the restaurant doesn't even really have a name, just "the VIP restaurant" of that company.

It's a pretty believable story, right? My parents never voiced any doubts about whether it's true. I think they never doubted it. But anyway, in Thai culture, we are taught, unlike Westerners, not to question things too much, especially if that questioning might lead to uncomfortable conclusions or discoveries. In fact, there is a Thai proverb warning people not to "think too much," that thinking too much only leads to unhappiness, and a loss of Buddhist balance in one's life. So in situations like this, not only did my parents not find out what I was up to, but they didn't want to find out. I think that kind of situation is not particular only to Thailand—sometimes you just don't want to know the full, real truth, especially when your daughter is giving handjobs for money!

As for me, I was not too disturbed about the particulars of working in the kapoo shop. I actually liked the "Harajuku Girls" concept, because it meant that I supposedly didn't speak Thai, and I didn't have to answer the customers' personal questions. And with heavy makeup and hair dying and the "Harajuku" costumes we wore, I thought it would be pretty unlikely that any man I knew would recognize me working there.

Being recognized was actually my only fear about working there. Giving handjobs to men—well, I'd done that for some boyfriends I'd had, so it wasn't all that terrible. It was in fact pretty terrible to have the slimy semen on my hands after each man, like squid paste, but at least I wasn't doing the full sex act, and I could wash my hands (over and over) after each customer. But what always perturbed me, and cause me to keep looking in the mirror and seeing how effective my "Japanese" makeup was, was the idea of some man I knew, probably an uncle or a restaurant customer or a boss (the customers were generally middle aged, so it wouldn't be a classmate or ex-boyfriend of mine), showing up there and recognizing me.

And I went really into my "Japanese" persona not only because it was being a good employee and helping the shop image and helping the man's fantasy of getting a handjob from a real Japanese girl, but also because it helped me place some distance between the real me and the Harajuku Girls me. At the end of the evening when I took off the costume and the makeup, and washed off the smell of semen on my hands (it does stay on after a lot of hand-washing, by the way), it provided me some separation and distance from that job. I was "Aki" (my name at the shop) and if the customers asked in broken Japanese or English about further details about my life, I only said I was from

Osaka and had been working in Bangkok for one month, and if they asked any more than that (usually in English), I pretended to be a combination of "shy" and "doesn't understand."

Did some of the customers know I wasn't really Japanese? Well, it's like did my parents know that I wasn't really working as a waitress. Thai people instinctively don't question things that are comfortable, and paradoxically, we Thai people do have a sense about when those comfortable things might be upset by too much questioning. So we don't want to question it too much because at some level we know that questioning it too much might reveal something uncomfortable. I would say that we are actually more perceptive than Westerners, who tend to question everything, and only after the questioning tend to realize that they've just revealed something that they might not have wanted to know in the first place!

So as far as I know, my customers never guessed that I wasn't Japanese. And as far as I could tell, none of them recognized me as Noi who used to work at the small restaurant in Pinklao. But they were Thai, and they didn't want to make those realizations after paying about 2,000 baht to be pleasured by a real Japanese girl from Osaka. So they didn't try too hard to break the whole experience. And in fact I know some other girls at Harajuku Girls did sometimes unintentionally break character, as I earlier mentioned, being unable to keep several acts going simultaneously, and suddenly speaking fluent Thai to their customers—I'm not sure how well their on-the-spot explanations for their sudden Thai language proficiency worked out. Though I obsessively scanned the Thai-language online discussion boards (pantip.com!) for mentions of Harajuku Girls, and especially any mentions of "Aki" (me), and I never read anything by anyone saying that they discovered we weren't really Japanese. Maybe they didn't want to lose face by admitting that they'd lost money on a not-really-Japanese "Japanese girl." Or maybe they went with the most comfortable version of events (there's that Thai trait again), and believed the girl's story that she's been taking Thai language classes in the mornings, or that her Japanese parents live and work in Bangkok, or that she has one Thai grandparent.

Most importantly for me, they never knew that Aki is Noi. In fact, one big reason you seldom find us Bangkok girls working in the sex trade is not just that Bangkok girls have more opportunity in life (especially opportunity to meet rich husbands), but also that we have more risk of our families and childhood friends seeing where we work. At Harajuku Girls, most of the girls were not from Bangkok, but the few us who were from Bangkok were always nervous about being recognized. (In fact, that's why some prostitution establishments do not allow Thai customers, although my Thai male friends just go in speaking English and saying they're from Hong Kong or Malaysia or the Philippines. The Harajuku Girls cheat all over again!)

In fact, it was the fear of being recognized that caused most of my stress at this job. I kept analyzing and checking and double and triple checking every customer's expressions and glances—they were just trying to get a good handjob, but I kept obsessing over whether they might possibly be recognizing me. The other thing that was getting to me was a sort of extreme anxiety about having sticky semen all over my hands about five times a day every work day. In fact, it dominated my thoughts more and more, and I thought made me less capable of doing a good job.

The customer and I would start the session by him showering, and me sometimes joining him in the shower if he was a little bit attractive or if he seemed like a big tipper. Otherwise, I'd shower by myself after he was done, and always instinctively washing and re-washing all the body parts that the day's (and more than the day's) customers had polluted with their semen and their saliva and their hands and their tongues.

I then helped the customer towel-dry himself, and led him to the bed, for the "massage," which of course isn't much of a massage. He'd lie face down and I'd sit beside him and give him a playful "massage" and maybe touch his nipples or his balls and giggle like a Japanese schoolgirl and pretend like it's the first time I've touched a guy *there*, which always improved his mood and I could see the cock always rising up and up around that moment. Or if it needed a little bit of help, I would open my kimono so he could see my breasts and pink nipples, and then definitely his cock would always be completely hard.

Then more playful massage, and then either when I wanted to finish things up, or when the customer couldn't take it any more, I would get the bottle of lotion, and still doing the "I'm not really sure what I'm doing here because I'm a shy innocent Japanese girl" act, awkwardly (or, fake awkwardly) squirt some lotion on his cock and make a ring with my fingers and rub it up and down. Then move my hand lightly around the very tip of the cock while moving up and down faster, which would always make the customer orgasm. Then act shocked and a bit scandalized by the semen, giggle something in fake Japanese, and go wash my hands.

I never got up to offering the customers anything more than a handjob ("upselling" it's called in English) I think because I didn't want to get too deeply into the whole thing. It would be a bit of extra money (maybe 1,000 extra baht) but it just wasn't worth it to me, for my self-image and self-respect, and also for the idea that their semen was, yes, all over my hands, but at least not anywhere else.

I never got used to the messiness and smell of semen on my hands. Even when I went home in the late evening or went out on personal errands in the mornings, I would suddenly smell semen, probably just purely from my imagination, like a flashback. It sounds funny now, but it was actually quite traumatizing. And of course any time I saw any gooey food or drink I would think about what I'd had on my hands at work that day. Not pleasant. And I was a girl who didn't mind giving handjobs and blowjobs to boyfriends, of course because they were really my boyfriends and I loved them or at least liked them a lot, but having five different men's semen on my hands every day was not pleasant.

There was something else wrong with Harajuku Girls for me. It was its upside and also its downfall. We were "Japanese girls" of course, so we weren't allowed to speak Thai, nor say anything about our real Thai identities. That means that I had no chance to get one of the big benefits of working in a prostitution venue, or in fact in any job where a 19-year-old single Thai girl might work: finding boyfriends, or at least "sugar daddy" supporters, but ideally, dream husbands (well, I dreamed!). No male coworkers, and not allowed to fraternize with the male customers. Not a good situation.

You probably already know by now that a Thai girl's major method of economic and life success is by attracting the right husband. This is of course true for poor Thai girls, but it's even true for rich Thai girls, and yes, for so-so working-class small-restaurant-owning-family Thai girls like me. In fact, foreigners always see that Thai girls always look beautiful in public and are always properly polite ("reap roy" in Thai) in public. It's not because we're vain! And it's not because we enjoy the effort and discomfort of putting on makeup and wearing it in the tropical weather, or wearing high heels up and down the BTS (Bangkok public transportation) station's stairs.

I wasn't permitted to reveal to my customers that I'm Thai, and even could not take my phone into the room with the customer, and the customer had to leave his valuables (and phone) in a locker near the entrance, supposedly "to protect your valuables" but really in case we were going to break character and exchange our contact information. I didn't know of any cases of it personally, but I could imagine a girl not breaking character, pretending to be Japanese, and still somehow setting up private meetings with a customer (where she could charge him directly, instead of letting the shop make most of the money). In that way, having us be "Japanese girls" did help the shop a lot, because it made it very difficult for that kind of thing. But even for my purposes, not of running a competing kapoo business but of meeting rich men to date, the whole "Japanese" story and the strict rules about no contacts and no fraternizing with customers made it very, very difficult. And if you know anything about Thailand, you know that breaking an employer's rules can lead to "serious consequences," because any business owner must have connections to the mafia. So it's not like I could just give customers my phone number and tell them I'm not really Japanese and just quit my job if my boss found out. The boss, and probably her mafia buddies, knew not only my name and information, but the basic location and information of my family. So you can imagine why I didn't dare try to meet men this way, and as far as I know, none of my coworkers did either.

To meet men, I could have gone to work at another kapoo shop, one that didn't require me to pretend to be Japanese, and where I could openly speak Thai with the customers—in fact, the one where my friend worked, owned by the same boss as Harajuku Girls, was hiring, although it would be a long commute there and back every day. The main reason I didn't like that idea was that it not only would be more and more semen on my hands, but would also involve lots of chitchat and personal questions and a very real chance of, say, my uncle or my classmate's father walking into the shop and immediately recognizing me. The loss of face was pretty significant. I have only one family, only one social group of classmates. If they saw me working in a naughty massage shop, it would change things permanently.

Instead of another kapoo shop, I chose to work at a hostess bar, which from the perspective of an employee, is pretty much exactly tailored to what I wanted to do: chat with rich men and hope for them to become my "daddies." As an additional benefit, the hostess club didn't have me going home every night with the smell of semen on my hands. And from what I'd heard, the salary was pretty similar to the kapoo salary.

Hostess Hustle

I wasn't getting any opportunities at Harajuku Girls to meet and let's say "engage with" rich men, partly because I wasn't sure how rich many of our customers were, but mostly because we were not allowed to break character and admit we're Thai or say anything about ourselves. I started investigating working in a close cousin of kapoo shops: a "gentlemen's club" or "hostess club." It's a close cousin of kapoo shops because it also doesn't offer full sex (or officially doesn't offer it) and pitches girls who are "higher class" and "not prostitutes," as compared to the girls that work in prostitution venues. This is all in a setting for "gentlemen," meaning rich guys. I know that in America, "gentlemen's clubs" are strip clubs, usually frequented by working class guys getting drunk. In Bangkok, though, they are really more like clubs for gentlemen, or at least for rich men, dressed fashionably, and usually "happily married" and looking for a girlfriend, or sometimes, rarely, divorced and looking for a second (upgrade) wife.

The premise of a gentlemen's club in Thailand is that guys go in a group to drink expensive drinks and be pampered by pretty girls. The customers are similar to the kapoo shop's customers, but maybe a little bit richer. Usually there's a story being told by the management that the girls are "high class" or "university students" or some such, which is of course as false as it is in any other similar venue. The big lure for us girls to work in the hostess club is not so much the salary—which consists mostly of commissions and tips, and at around 30,000 baht a month is good but not spectacular—but to find "sugar daddies."

Going to a Thai gentleman's club is a way for a Thai man to announce "I've made it in the world, I have lots of money, and I'm looking for pretty girls to spend it on." Well, we, the hostesses at those clubs, are the pretty girls that they're looking for. Inside the club, we stare into their eyes and tell them how handsome they are, giggle at their jokes, look at the photos of their latest vacation (with their wife, of course), put our arms around them, and sometimes give them a grope or a peck on the cheek. In return, they're expected to "buy drinks" for us. Those "drinks" aren't really drinks, but a fee for us sitting with them. Of course, you know that we Thai people don't like to rudely put out the naked truth (other than what I'm doing in this book!) so we never say that we're charging a fee just for sitting with them, but we only want them to "buy us a drink."

Typically, the drink costs about 200 to 300 baht (so $7-10 dollars), and we are instructed by management that each drink should last no more than 30 minutes. Actually if we've been playing the customer well, we can make each drink last no more than 30 seconds. That's what makes a successful, high-earning (both for herself and for the club) hostess girl.

After the drink is done, we ask for another drink. Or not directly ask, but point and pout a little bit at the empty or near-empty glass. And what man can deny buying a drink for a pretty girl? When I really got into the game, I was able to get the customer more aroused, and dropping some sexual hints, just as the drink was running out, to ensure he'd buy one more. So the drinks keep coming, and the bartender knows to mostly give us colored water that smells a bit like alcohol, because no hostess girl likes to actually drink ten or more alcoholic drinks in one evening.

At the place where I worked, the girls' drinks cost 250 baht each, and our commission from each drink was 100 baht. Officially, anyway. In reality, the floor manager (the "mama") often took away some of that as her *own* commission for introducing a customer to us or encouraging him to drink more or bringing him a drink or just when she felt like it. Well, she knew that for the most part, we wouldn't and couldn't do anything about it. Although often I, like my coworkers, just felt like I wanted to scream at the customer "just give me money directly! don't buy drinks because I won't get paid from that!" but I couldn't do that, and that would break the illusion of me sitting there because the guy is so enchanting, and not because I'm getting paid for it.

At the end of a session for a group of customers, there was the point of tipping. And usually in Thailand, there's no tipping (at least not for Thai people; expectations are different for foreigners), but for a hostess club, there's some tipping expected. Usually the customer will leave the tip inside his bill folder, just like in a restaurant. What the customer doesn't realize is that when he walks out the door, the mama (manager) will grab that tip money, and maybe give us girls a hundred baht here or there, but most of it will be for her, not for us—unless she specifically likes us, or, as was the case in the place where I worked, one of the girls is her niece!

So where's the sex, you might be thinking? There's no sex at most hostess clubs. There wasn't any sex inside the hostess club where I worked, though I've heard there are some more "elite" hostess clubs that have private karaoke rooms where you can have sex with the girls, for very high prices, something like 10,000 baht just to get into the private room. And of course the customers are told "I'm only doing this for you because you're so special." At the club where I worked, there's no sex inside the club, but of course we had men spending money, and we were arousing those men every way we could for an entire evening, and here are some pretty girls touching and hugging them and those pretty girls by the way are in need of money.... of course something is going to come of this. (Oops, I just made a pun.)

As I mentioned, I worked in a hostess club to try to foster sugar daddy and long term boyfriend relationships, ideally a long-term, monogamous, dependable husband. Having a "daddy," and that's not a biological father, is a pretty common for thing for young pretty Thai girls. I know that Westerners are disgusted by the idea and it's too close to incest, but in Thai culture, it's not unusual to colloquially refer to your husband or boyfriend as your dad, and remember that we even call the King and monks our fathers. (Similarly to how Catholics call priests "father.") My long-term goal was of course marriage to a rich man, but until that appeared, I would be happy with having a "daddy," or a few of them.

So I was on the search for a daddy. What kind of daddy? One who could "donate" maybe at least 10,000 baht per month to me, regularly, that I could pass on to my family. Or 20,000 baht per month, which some girls could get, but I think they needed to be very expert at being mistresses to be making 20,000 baht a month. What would a girl like me have to do in exchange for that money? Just being an older guy's girlfriend and making him feel good, basically the same routine as we did inside the club, just outside the club, going out with his friends wherever he wanted, or sometimes getting a hotel room together for a night of sex. (It would be rare to actually go to the guy's home, as almost all of them are married, or if they're not married, they wouldn't want to be seen by neighbors or relatives with their private sexual encounters.)

And that 20,000 baht a month, "only" about $600 for Americans, would make a huge difference for my family. It would replace the money we used to make from the restaurant, which was now, after the fire and after a branch of MK opened nearby, not even breaking even. While my parents had rebuilt the restaurant as best they could, it didn't look or smell very nice, and business was declining, not just because of the fire damage, nor because of the new nearby competition, but because it is considered bad luck in Thai culture to frequent a place that has had a fire occur there. Because of that bad luck, some of our regular customers stopped coming, and because everyone knew about the fire and the bad luck, we also couldn't sell or rent the house, because no one would want to pay much money for an unlucky place like that. My parents couldn't really do much else other than run the restaurant, and didn't have any good skills that could get them a significant salary. Anyway, in Thailand, unlike in America, age discrimination isn't considered discrimination, just a normal way of hiring, and most jobs openly say they don't want to hire anyone over about 35.

I started looking for a "daddy" because my dream was to be able to appear in my parents' doorway once a month with a stack of 1,000 baht bills, and them to smile and tell me what a good daughter I am, and their lives being easier because of it—this is not such a ridiculous dream, is it? Please tell me it's not, because it's the dream of almost every girl in Thailand. And if it involved making an older rich guy feel good and going on some expensive dinner dates and maybe even hotel nights with him, it's really not so bad.

You may have heard, if you are a tourist, especially a sex tourist, in Thailand, that Thai girls love older men or that age differences don't matter in Thailand. That's totally, totally, 100% untrue! Thai girls want guys their own age (usually ideally about 5 years older) just like every other girl. No, we twentysomething Thai girls don't lust after 60+ year old men, and usually not even 40+ year old men. But you often see bargirls with much older customers and boyfriends and even husbands, right? Yes, sure. And it's true that many Thai girls, especially bargirls, choose to marry much older foreigners. But that is only because they have no better option in life. It's not that they love senior men. It's that considering everything together (including money), that's the best they can do. And as a side benefit, an old man is likely not to demand too much sex or any other kind of activity, and might even die soon and leave his wife his condo and his money!

So if you take that to mean that old foreign men are "desirable" in Thailand, then yes, I guess so, they are desirable by bar girls because they are less demanding and they are more likely to die on that girl's watch, and without a horde of Thai relatives to swoop down on the leftover money, as would be the case when an old Thai man dies.

But don't think, or at least if you want the naked truth and not some comfortable fairy tales, that we Thai girls just love old men or don't mind age. When I was fishing for a "daddy" at the hostess club, of course I would have preferred to have been chosen as a girlfriend by a rich 25 year old guy, instead of merely having to be a mistress for a 50 year old guy. I would have liked it a million times more. But my looks are only "cute" or "slightly above average," not supermodel status. And a rich 25 year old guy in Thailand can and does get supermodel status girls, not "kind of cute" girls like me. So as much as I can dream about rich 25 year old guys, they would not be dreaming about me. And the "daddies" at the hostess club were my best option.

One night I heard the entrance door opening, and when I looked over, I thought I saw a good candidate walking in. 180 cm (almost 6 feet) tall, blue oxford shirt, neat slacks, very expensive polished designer shoes, and visibly showing off a BMW car key in his hand. I had never previously seen or at least noticed him at the club. He had a certain well-mannered ease. He walked into the hostess club as if he owned it, but being the politest owner possible. I remember that his collar had those expensive metal clips on it (I don't even know what they're called), not plastic buttons, and his sleeves also had cufflinks. He said it was his first time there (who knows if that was true). But as soon as he walked in, I noticed him scanning the room full of girls, then looking only at me. I was wearing a particularly tight black sheer dress that evening, and it really showed off my slim body and long white-skinned legs. He smiled and nodded for me to sit with him as he sat down with a group of other men who were already drinking and playing dice games.

His name was Aek. And he said he's a lawyer who works for Thai Airways. This was by way of introduction. That might be a bit forward for a casual introduction in the Western world, but in the Thai world, an introduction has to carry some signals about status and rank, because, of course, Thai society is built on the idea of rank. And while Americans would consider the idea offensive, a Thai person thinks it's only natural that you should know how rich someone is so you know how to treat them appropriately!

For us hostess girls, of course, the goal was a lot less abstract than following Thai social protocol, although very compatible and maybe observationally equivalent with it: ascertaining who would be a good "daddy." A young guy coming in to have some fun might be great for making some drink commissions and maybe a tip, but he wouldn't serve our longer-term goal of finding a good financial sponsor for life, or at least for longer than one day. A young rich guy also usually had too many options: especially if he was single, his family was already setting him up with lots of girls who were every bit as beautiful as hostess club girls, but from much higher class backgrounds. And you know that class means everything in Thailand. Meanwhile, an older married man could not be presented as a suitor to young rich girls looking for a husband, and has to resort to girls like us, pretty girls not from the richest backgrounds, who are willing to be "on the side" or whatever else, for a good "daddy."

Aek was prospectively a perfect "daddy" for a girl like me. I liked his look, but more importantly, it was obvious that he'd come from generations of wealth. At the upper levels of Thai society, it's not so much one's salary or job that matters, but family wealth and power that's been built up over generations. And in fact the reason why his being a lawyer for Thai Airways sounded so great was not because the salary of that job is good but because to have that job, you must come from the "right" background, and the right background is a rich background. That's why we hostess girls will sometimes ooh and ahh at Thai guys who tell us they have jobs that aren't high paying—for example, a professor of literature at Chulalongkorn University (the best university in Thailand) earns a salary smaller than a hostess girl's salary, but to be socially allowed to have that job, a man has to be from a rich family. It's not that we're interested in a literature professor's 20,000 baht a month ($600 USD) monthly salary, but that having that job is a marker of big family wealth. In Thailand, your birth and family wealth pretty much limit what jobs you are permitted to have. If you are from a poor background, even if somehow you managed to get an excellent education (perhaps you had a benefactor who took

you outside of Thailand to get an education), once you came back to
Thailand, you would not be permitted to work in a top-level university.
It's simply considered improper.

That's why for girls like me, from working-class backgrounds, there
isn't that much opportunity other than jobs like being a hostess, and
most importantly, trying to marry and "follow in the coattails of" a rich
guy like Aek. My family background is nothing remarkable, and even
if somehow I managed to, say, get a PhD or a medical degree, it would
be impossible for me to get a top-rate job in Thailand. People would
laugh at the idea of someone with no family pedigree being a professor
or a doctor, no matter what degrees I had. For that reason, there's not
much reason for a girl like me to pursue higher education in Thailand,
and that's why I did not pursue any higher education until I arrived in
America. Also, the logical conclusion is not only that someone with no
pedigree can't get a high-level job, but also that anyone with a high-level
job must have a family pedigree. For a hostess girl, who is trying to land
a guy with a lot of family money, this means any guy with a top-level
job also has a lot of family money (and power) standing behind him.
That makes things easier than in the first world, where you might meet
a guy who has a high-level job, but has so much debt and zero wealth
that he can't do much for you materially. At least in Thailand, kind of
perversely, you can be sure that anyone with a "high-respect" job, even
if that job has a low salary (or a low official salary), has a lot of family
wealth, property, and influence.

In Aek's case, and it made me full of hope and anticipation, he had
not only a prestigious job, but a high-paying prestigious job, suggesting
not only a big salary, but big family wealth. That is, of course, jackpot
time for a girl looking for a "daddy," and even more so when looking for
a husband.

That first evening with Aek and his friends was almost
uncomfortable, because I was so nervous about myself, and lacking
confidence in front of this bigshot whom of course I was trying to

impress. Every time I went to run my fingers over his facial stubble, it felt so unnatural and forced and awkward to me—although it might not have been too bad, because he was enjoying it, and at some point in the evening, he opened his day-planner notebook, with its pen inside, and asked me to write down my phone number. He wrote "Noi" (using English letters!) next to my phone number. Noi is such a common name that I childishly, girlishly felt very special, thinking for a half-second that I'm the only Noi in his life! I don't think so. Even at that time, I didn't think so.

And that one evening, I worked hard at keeping just the right amount of temptation and sexual tension, to keep him interested, but not give him everything he wants. I ran my hand over his stubble, I held his hand for a split-second, I blew in his ear, but I never let his hand travel too much over my body, and I never kissed him. I think it's a good middle way. In fact, this middle way is the key to success in the hostess club, my coworkers always told me. Your goal is to keep the guy coming back, and outside the club, keep him buying you things, never believing that you're completely *his*, because then he takes you for granted and the wallet closes. But so what. I wanted to be *his*, at least Aek's. I wouldn't have objected at all being his fulltime girlfriend, stopping all the teasing and giving him the whole Noi package, even if the financial support it got my family would be modest, because he was not a crazy seventy-year-old billionaire or a spend-happy twenty something gangster, just a reliable and well-off fortysomething lawyer with clear aristocratic roots.

I liked him, just that first night, in the most irrational, Western-style, romantic way, even beyond his financial stability and his supposed ability to support me. But my rational, family-supporting side also liked him, and not only because I could see he has money, but because I could see he is calm and cool and collected, a man I would want to let into my life. In Thai we say someone is "jai yen," which in English would literally translate to "cold-hearted," which I know means something bad in English—but in Thai, it's the utmost compliment, meaning that someone "keeps his cool under pressure." Every Thai woman wants a husband who is "jai yen." That's a good boy. The opposite would be a man who is "jai lon," "hot-hearted," impulsive and perhaps violent. Do bargirls tell you that Thai men are jai lon (hot-hearted, have a bad temper)? It's not because all Thai men are jai lon. But it's because all the jai yen men have been snapped up by girls more desirable than bargirls. (And yes, in Thai society, hostess girls are way, way more desirable than bargirls, even separately from the obvious differences in usual skin color.)

Aek was super duper jai yen, the way every woman wants. And that would make him a good partner and potentially a good husband, but as I found, it would also make it difficult to really play him for money or affection, as he absolutely could not be made to act impulsively or irrationally. In my meetings with him, the dinners, the Peninsula-Hotel "overnight dates," and yes, even the hours of sexual ecstasy, I could not get him to for once drop everything, drop his rationality, and commit to me completely.

I kept searching for the magic thing to say, the magic dress to wear, the magic sexual position to try, even the magic jealousy-inducing comment to make, to get him to commit to me completely, emotionally, make me his only his girlfriend, even his wife. But he was too calm and cool and collected, always scanning the situation with his very "jai yen" brown eyes, his face and mouth never revealing any emotion other than "oh, yes, I see, I will keep that in mind."

Even when he orgasmed—his favorite position was to take me from behind, he said because he loved to look at my long white back with my black hair on it—he never lost control, never had the "little death" that orgasm is supposed to be, only seemed to have a good half-minute of very controlled pleasure. Everything I tried in the bedroom, every new blowjob move I tried to do, he enjoyed and appreciated, but it never got me to the tipping point of him completely giving himself to me. It is a truism among Thai women, and sometimes even whispered to us by our mothers, that it is by sexual skill that we can get men to completely embrace us and stop thinking about us only rationally. Do you see the shadows of Buddhism and the idea of finding yourself by losing yourself? And there's also the idea that marriage is a gamble, because traditionally, you are not having sex with the man before the wedding, and it is only after the wedding when you have sex, and when you try to make him completely commit to you. When a man loses interest in a woman after marriage, it is always rumored behind the scenes in traditional Thai families that maybe her sexual skills weren't good enough, maybe her mother didn't teach her right.

Was I not good enough in bed? Or was Aek too much a cool customer? He split his time, and most of his money, between his legal wife, with whom he had a son and also a real estate business, and his #1 girlfriend, who was also his secretary at his law office. In Thai slang, that's a "mia yai" (big wife) and "mia noi" (small wife). I was ranked even lower than a mia noi for him, and I feared that all I could aspire to for him was mia noi status, not becoming a mia yai, the real wife. "Work" was always his effective excuse for spending time with one woman or the other. Aren't lawyers good at coming up with excuses? Not that he had any obligation to make excuses for me—I was after all, only somewhere down the line of girlfriends, maybe still in the single digits in the numbering system, I could hope—but the concept of "work" could give him a smooth way to say "with wife or #1 girlfriend" without broaching any decidedly un-Thai semblance of breaking social harmony.

Of course I kept working at the hostess club while I was seeing Aek. My attempts at making him jealous never succeeded. I'd mention that so-and-so general or government minister or police chief or CEO was my customer at the hostess club and asked me out that very evening but that I turned him down to spending the evening seeing (and sexually pleasuring) Aek. And Aek's response was never "Oh! So kind of you!"

or "Wow, what if next time you choose the other guy?!" but more like "Well, of course, it would be silly to choose any other man over me!" That confidence made him sexy to me, but also made it difficult to rein him in or make him definitely commit.

I was devoting most of my free time outside the club to courting Aek. And it really did feel like I was courting him, and not he was courting me. Of course, that makes sense, since there are more young poor pretty girls in Thailand than there are bigshots like Aek. And as any courter knows, I was going after the big prize, marriage or a solid relationship, but as time went on with Aek, I realized more and more that this prize was completely out of reach.

He did spend money on me, but an expensive dinner, even a LV handbag (which I could cash in by posting it for sale on Facebook once he stopped asking me whether I like it), or an occasional wad of 1,000 baht notes left in my purse, didn't do much for my long-term financial situation, or my family's security. The 5,000 baht gifts of course helped me and my parents a lot, but they were not something to build a life on. And I wanted something to build a life on, not just occasional short-term assistance. I knew very well that this kind of relationship I had with Aek could end at any second. He liked me, we enjoyed spending time together, he thought I was cute, but I don't think he was particularly head-over-heels infatuated with me, and he knew very well that girls like me are "a dime a dozen." (Are we really? I think I'm more special than that, but I think I didn't quite realize it until later.)

My times with other customers at the hostess club were basically an echo, on a smaller scale, of my times with Aek. They did spend money buying me drinks at the club, but of course that was just making the boss rich, not doing anything for me directly. And they did take me out, sometimes on sex dates, with expensive dinners and shoe or bag shopping, and that's enjoyable for a girl in her early twenties, but it's not a way to secure a long-term life. When I felt that a customer was really "into" me, when I saw he kept staring at me, or looking especially at my lithe fair-skinned body, it could lead to a few thousand baht in the club, then maybe a few ten thousands of baht outside the club, but it never turned into anything more than that. I felt myself becoming a little bit desperate about this. When having sex with a CEO or government minister in a hotel room, I'd sometimes even drop a hint like "maybe next time we can go to your place?" and I was always met with the smile that Thai people give to say "are you out of your fucking mind?" Well, maybe I was out of my fucking mind, wanting a husband and stability for my good looks which were not set to last that long, not only an LV bag and expensive dinners.

I couldn't go on and on like that for years and years, and I couldn't expect the money to keep coming in, because once a girl reaches 25 or 26 or 27, the clubs don't want to hire her anymore. And it's not because the clubs specifically don't like slightly older girls, but it's because for the customers, being with a girl who's coming up on 30 is too close to their real lives, probably in the age range of their wives (usually our customers would be in their 50s and their wives would be in their 30s) not the escapist fantasy that the "gentlemen's club" promises. We all claim to be 20 or 21 or 22 in the club, of course, to keep the fantasy going, just as we claimed to be "Japanese" at Harajuku Girls. When you're 25, you can pull it off. When you're 30, maybe not.

So as I was brushing married men's stubble and playing with their hair and blowing into their ears at the hostess club, I was definitely thinking about how to get to a new job, one better suited for making a long-term plan. I knew there were openings in some hostess clubs, and in fact, some of the new hostess clubs were desperate for girls and were even paying 70% commissions on drinks to entice new employees. I was also pitched the idea of working in an "ab nam" ("bath") establishment, which is a straight-up brothel primarily for Thai men, where you bathe your customer and then have sex with him. I threw away the ab nam idea because I knew that while the money could be good, I'd have to service about five customers a day, and had no say in the matter, could not turn away customers, and pretty much had to do as the customers ordered. That was very different from Harajuku Girls, where I always had the fallback position of "sorry, I can't do that, this is only a handjob shop" and of course "sorry, I don't understand Thai," and of the hostess club, where I could act shocked that a customer would proposition a hostess for sex! No, in the ab nam world, famous palaces like Poseidon on Ratchada Road, there was no cover story, no fallback position, no turning away customers, and no telling myself (or my family) that I was anything but a prostitute. So, just no.

As the "dark horse candidate" in my job consideration, I heard about the foreigner-oriented bar districts, such as Soi Cowboy and Nana Plaza. I'd heard rumblings from acquaintances that now there were some openings for "premium" bargirls in the infamous farang-oriented stripper bars on Soi Cowboy. Why "premium" bargirls? For Thai girls who know a little bit about sex work in Bangkok, working on Soi Cowboy is seen as something for very ugly, very dark-skinned (in Thai culture, synonymous with ugly), older girls, usual who have a few kids back in Issan. Oh yes, and it's something for girls from Issan.

For Bangkok Thai guys, dark skin or an Issan accent makes a Thai girl untouchable, or bottom of the barrel. So Issan girls, and their working places, are kind of on the bottom of the hierarchy for Thai girls working in the "body business" (one Thai euphemism for sex work). It makes their working places, like Soi Cowboy, considered equally untouchable. And so not only are white-skinned Bangkok girls (like your correspondent, Noi) considered higher-class by Thai people, but we Bangkok girls ourselves generally believe ourselves too good to be working in places like Soi Cowboy. We're a "premium" product in relation to Soi Cowboy, and so our job on Soi Cowboy would also be "premium."

Premium or not, the most important things about the opportunity for Soi Cowboy were that my uncles or classmates certainly wouldn't see me there (I didn't have any farang uncles or classmates!), I could turn away customers and pretend to be "only a dancer," and maybe most importantly, it was well known inside and even outside the sex trade that working as a bargirl in the farang districts often led to marrying a foreigner. What *kind* of foreigner, and how good the marriage, well, that varied a lot, and of course Thai people like to snicker at those marriages, but anyway, marriage was a real option—an option that I was becoming increasingly certain I would never be presented by the men I had met at the gentlemen's club. And Aek? I think even setting foot on Soi Cowboy, even if as a premium coyote dancer girl, would make me ineligible to even be one of his side girlfriends—but I was fine with losing that low-hanging fruit if it helped me toward my pursuit of the big goal.

Night after night, I was getting very tired of big talk and little long-term security from the hostess-club guys. It was quick cash with no long-term hopes. It was ok for a young girl, fresh out of high school or not much older, but it was not a way to sustain a long-term living. It was, despite my hopes to the contrary, very unlikely to lead to a stable, long-term relationship with a guy, it would make me unmarriageable to any good Thai guy anyway, and once I reached about 28, I wouldn't even be eligible to be a hostess. Not even that.

Yes, thanks to the hostess bar, I was playing with rich guys every night. But it was only playing, and they, like Aek, definitely were only playing. And they didn't seem to realize that I wasn't the owner of the hostess club. I was getting only a tiny cut of the money they were spending on drinks and snacks. And they didn't seem to realize that this was my job, my way to make money. What I mean is that they thought that I am delighted to meet them and talk with them. And that they buy me a few drinks and I should be happy with having some free whiskey. Not really realizing that I'm not there to drink free whiskey with a middle-aged bigshot, but to make some money for me and my family, and ideally, to find long-term security. And that promise of finding long-term security—really only available through marriage for a regular Thai girl—is what brought me to working in Soi Cowboy.

Hierarchy of Flesh

Soi Cowboy is an alley ("soi" in Thai) right in the middle of downtown Bangkok. It's full of neon signs, drunk foreign men, and dark-skinned girls from Issan stripping and dancing. The general setup is that we girls dance on a stage, and our customers can "buy us drinks," which is a polite way of giving us tips, because, just as in the hostess club, we make a big commission from drinks. Or, if they really like us, they can "take us home." Sometimes foreign men are shy and call it "going out to dinner," but of course it's going out for sex, either in a rented room somewhere nearby, or back at the customer's hotel room. That's what happens in Soi Cowboy thousands of times every night, every night of the year, for many years now. They say that Soi Cowboy got its name because it originally had only one bar, and the owner of the bar was an American guy who walked around in a cowboy hat. Many Thai people don't even know this place exists, but it's a top attraction for foreigners coming to Thailand.

And among Thai people who know about it, especially Thai girls in the body business, it's considered kind of a joke, kind of a low-class place, even among prostitution places. Imagine how "respectable" people look down on prostitutes. Well that's how kapoo/hostess/massage prostitutes look down on Soi Cowboy prostitutes! Why? Largely because the Soi Cowboy girls are dark-skinned and generally already have a few children back home, and are considered ugly and undesirable by Thai men. But that's only half the reason. The other half of the reason is from envy or "sour grapes" as Americans say. Those delicious grapes are... foreign men who are willing to marry and completely commit to a prostitute. Make her the #1 in their lives. Marry her without any reservations about her past. Let her completely become a new person, a wife, when she used to be a prostitute. A Thai man would never do that. Maybe it's because Thai people believe you carry karma (Buddhist virtue) built up over generations and lifetimes, and there's no easy way to get rid of it, so in Thai culture, if you're a prostitute, even if your ancestor was a prostitute, you're "marked" and evil. Western culture, on the other hand, believes that a person is new, can make themselves born new, like the Buddhist concept of a completely clean rebirth.

But our subject here is survival economics, not theology or religious history. The point is, if you are a "working girl," you're unlikely to find a lifelong commitment from a Thai man. A nightly commitment, absolutely. A monthly commitment, sure. Even being "on his list" for a lifetime is possible. A Thai man can even make you a lifetime gik ("gik" is Thai slang for a fuckbuddy), with some nice meals and LV bags, but not a lifetime wife, not the real security a woman always wants.

Another big advantage of the farang (foreigner) bars on Soi Cowboy compared to the hostess clubs was that I could make things completely clear about money. A hostess club and a Soi Cowboy bar are really just the same thing, a place for meeting prostitutes, but a hostess club takes more steps to hide it. It would be completely out of place in a hostess club for a guest to ask a hostess girl "how much for sex?" or even "how much for two hours of you sitting on my face?" even though everyone knows that is exactly what both customers and girls are thinking. At Soi Cowboy, those questions are asked, openly, every day. Sometimes the shy, younger customers, often Americans, would say something like "I'd like to spend time with you." But the older men, and especially Europeans, would describe the sex they wanted to have with a lot of detail, sometimes with English even worse than mine at the time. Either way, I could quote a price, and I wouldn't need to waste money having dinner and the whole time anxiously wondering how much he'd pay me or whether I'd have to be satisfied with just sharing a nice dinner and expensive wine. It got rid of the uncertainty and the game of the hostess club. Meanwhile, the advantage of Soi Cowboy over the Ratchada Road "bath massage" brothels is that I kept all the money I made, I could turn down customers if I didn't want to go home with them, and I'd be expected to "go home with" maybe 1-2 customers a night, not 5-6 like they do at the Ratchada Road massage baths.

The downside of working at Soi Cowboy? It is really considered the bottom end of the Bangkok body business, and normally, my parents would be beyond mortified (if there is such a thing!) for my working in any place like that. Of course, they'd be mortified anyway if I worked in any sort of prostitution. So let me rephrase. I think even my friends who work in the body business, like my friend Tam who brought me to work at Harajuku Girls, would look down on working at Soi Cowboy. It was dirty. It was full of Isaan girls and dirty old foreigners. I knew that if Aek—who was still my part-time "daddy," but who seemed to be drifting away more and more to the world of his #1 girlfriend, his secretary—found out that I worked at Soi Cowboy, he'd drift away from me even faster than he'd been doing up until that point.

I didn't even know anyone who worked on Soi Cowboy. I had never been there, other than when I would sometimes walk to Terminal 21, a shopping mall near Soi Cowboy, and would glance over at Soi Cowboy and think to myself "glad I'm not working there!" But one of my coworkers from the hostess club knew a woman who co-owned one of the bars on Soi Cowboy, and told me that it's actually not such a bad place to work, and that white-skinned Bangkok girls like me would get higher pay and better treatment. We'd be "premium." Moreover, and this was something so obvious to any Thai girl that it doesn't need to be said, but both my hostess coworker and the bar owner felt the need to reiterate it: there's a good chance of being married off to a foreigner! And maybe, if I was a "high class" girl, it would be a "high class" foreigner, not the penniless tattooed seventy-year-old Australian retirees (Thai slang: "farang kee nok," bird shit foreigners) that we imagined bargirls marrying? I hadn't been able to get Aek to commit to me, and my real Thai dating prospects were pretty much nonexistent if

I worked as a hostess girl, so I did want to try the Soi Cowboy route, even if I surprised even myself.

Remember that I mentioned that I'd be a "premium" girl and have a "premium" job at Soi Cowboy? Soi Cowboy reserves a "premium" job title, "coyote dancer," and not just plain bargirl, for the "premium girls." The coyote dancers are generally Bangkok girls who are hesitant, as I was, about working on Soi Cowboy. Thai society is all about hierarchy and place, and normally, Soi Cowboy is not the proper place for a Bangkok girl. But the job title of a coyote dancer makes it proper. Moreover, officially anyway, a coyote dancer is not a prostitute, and not having sex with the customers. Just like officially, hostess girls and kapoo massage girls are not having sex with the customers! Of course we were having sex with the customers in all those situations, but you remember what I said about deniability and cover stories and Thai culture not encouraging Thai people to question comfortable beliefs.

In the Soi Cowboy bar, we had two tiers of girls. One was "bargirls," and they were kind of the Isaan girls you normally associate with the world of Soi Cowboy. All the customers knew that these girls were available for taking home. If one of these girls didn't want to be taken home by a certain customer, she could always either quote the customer a ridiculous price (say, 10,000 baht, about $300), or say that she has her period or that she has to visit her mother tonight or something like that. But she couldn't say "bargirls don't go home with customers," because that would be too ridiculous even for a Thai face-saving lie! That was for the bargirls. For the premium, "coyote dancer" girls (about 20% of the girls in the bar), like me, there was a thicker veneer of "we're not prostitutes."

We're not prostitutes! We're only dancers! Sure. Well, that is in fact the line we used when a customer who was not very appealing wanted to take us out for sex. And by "very appealing," I don't mean physical appeal. Remember we Thai women are practical! Not to mention that Soi Cowboy is our work and our livelihood, not leisure time as it is for foreign tourists. And remember that the primary appeal of working on Soi Cowboy is not so much the salary or the tips or even the sex fees. It's the opportunity to meet a long-term husband. Or at the very least, a "supporting boyfriend" of the kind that Aek was for me from the hostess club. But, if we were lucky, the "supporting boyfriend" would, unlike Aek, not have many other options for attention and affection and sex, so we girls would be the ones controlling the situation.

I came to work at 5 P.M. on my first day at the bar, which is when the owner told me to come. 5 P.M. was also work start time at the hostess club, so it fit into my schedule, and it felt like I was just continuing my life, except getting off the BTS (Bangkok public transit) at a different stop, the one for Soi Cowboy (Asok station) instead of the one for the hostess club (Ekkamai station). When I showed up at 5 P.M., fresh from the BTS and hesitantly waiting to be introduced to Soi Cowboy, the bar wasn't open at all, and I got funny looks when I was knocking on all its side doors. I had to call the owner's mobile phone to ask her to come and meet me there. She sent a motorcycle taxi to pick me up and bring me to her "office," a small shophouse a few streets away, actually appearing quite similar to my parents' restaurant where I had grown up.

The boss, Ms. Chiraporn, looked like the auntie I had expected her to look like. In fact, she looked like one of my aunts so much that I was filing through my head making sure she was not in fact a relative of mine, but once I listened to her voice, I decided that I'd never before met her. She asked me my details—I had actually been hired without any details, just my name and age and a photo of my ID card that I sent her through Whatsapp, and another photo of me "looking good." After my initial "interview," over Whatsapp, she had sent me a cursory message saying that ok, I'm hired, and the base salary is 20,000 baht a month. I knew that already, and I knew that the real money didn't lie in the base salary, and the really big opportunity was in the extra fees and most importantly in the lonely foreigners I'd meet. Now she was covering more detailed questions like, whether I had any children, whether I had any boyfriends, whether I used drugs. *No* to all three questions. The questions went on and mostly were trying to find if I was going to bring any trouble to her establishment. Did I have any enemies in Bangkok? Did I ever have any sexual diseases? No to both. Could I speak English? Actually my English was not so bad, thanks to high school and TV shows and the internet, and I surprised the boss when I was able to keep up with her in her attempt at English conversation with me. The "premium" girls on Soi Cowboy usually are "premium" in everything but their English ability—they don't come from the Issan world of "you have to learn English to find a foreign husband" and usually have Thai boyfriends, so their English is not so good. But my English was good, and this made me a good prospect for the bar owner—although also potentially dangerous, in a "she knows too much" kind of way.

Next in my meeting with the bar boss: costumes. Outfits. Compulsory on Soi Cowboy. At the hostess club, we had some tips from the bosses and our coworkers about what kinds of outfits to wear, but there was no uniform. Here, there was a uniform for the coyote dancers. Actually, there were a few uniforms, one for each day of the week. I know Westerners, especially girls, don't like uniforms. But for me, and I think also for my coworkers at the bar, uniforms make life easy. Not only do we not have to worry about what to wear, but we don't have to compete with our coworkers, nor do we have to worry about matching our coworkers. It's all done for us. In fact, even many white-collar jobs in Thailand require employees to wear uniforms.

Uniforms are important to us Thais because in addition to the benefits that are obvious to Westerners, such as not having to choose what to wear, they make it easier for us to distinguish who is who in the hierarchy of any workplace, even the hierarchy among bar employees. You probably know that for Thai people, every social interaction has to do with relationships in a hierarchy. Well, even for prostitutes in a bar on Soi Cowboy, there's a lot of hierarchy. And not following the proper hierarchical protocol can lead to loss of face for everyone. Uniforms make it easy to know who's who, and in the case of my time on Soi Cowboy, they made it easy to distinguish who is a regular bargirl, who is a "coyote dancer" (like me), and who is a waitress. And the only woman in the bar not wearing a uniform is always the boss.

Of course, coyote dancers are "higher class" than the regular bargirls, so our uniforms were also "higher class." For every evening, they focused on fantasy themes, like flight attendants or nurses or police officers. Meanwhile, the regular bar girls' uniforms were just a matter of showing the most body possible, not following a fantasy theme. Of course, that serves to mark the hierarchy, and also make the coyote girls higher-class, more unattainable, more out-of-reach. In reality, it was a funny result, because our bodies definitely looked better than the bar girls' bodies, but we showed a lot less of our bodies than they did—we were generally younger, whiter-skinned, and didn't have the marks of childbearing and farm labor that almost all of the Isaan girls that worked as regular bargirls carried. They needed to show a lot of skin. For us, the "premium" girls, it was enough to show just a little bit of skin.

I was fitted for my set of uniforms. The boss's hired seamstress buzzed around, measuring me and trying different pieces on me. The fit was of course more for looks than for comfort, and I wasn't surprised that they were going to make the shorts extra-tight to emphasize my firm butt (unlike many of the other girls, I had never had kids!) and the torso top extra short to show off my white skin and my flat stomach. There were five uniforms, for five variations—nurse, teacher, flight crew, police, and black leather. They all fit the same way, and were really the same garments other than the outside decorations, so one fitting session was all I needed for the whole set. While the seamstress worked on that day's uniform, the boss told me more about the specifics of the job, none of which was a surprise to me, as I'd been asking around and collecting at least second- or third- hand information.

Most important to the boss was that I would come to work on time. At 7:00 P.M., I was to be already in my uniform and ready to dance on the stage. If I was late even by a minute, my pay would be decreased. She also told me that I always had to be pushing customers to buy drinks for themselves and for me; I answered that I had worked in a hostess bar, so I knew this routine very well, and she gave me a knowing nod. She also told me what I knew about going home with customers: that I should making as much of those 700 baht "go home fees" ("bar fines") as possible, but that if I absolutely don't want some customer, I could always say that coyote girls don't go with customers.

She asked me whether I'd ever performed on a stage or done any kind of dancing. I said that at the hostess club, sometimes all the girls would dance on the stage during slow times, but I wasn't one of the show or dancer girls. Of course I could dance at bars with my friends, but that seemed a world apart from dancing in front of farangs in a Soi Cowboy bar. Ms. Chiraporn (my new boss) said that it wasn't much of a skill and I wouldn't have to be much of a dancer, just look beautiful and smile at the customers.

And then she let out a little bit of a smile and said that years ago, she also worked in a hostess bar, and she knows that I'd be a good worker and a good saleswoman for her. She said she was from Samut Prakan, near Bangkok, which also gave her some affinity with me, as we were among the few bar staff not from Issan. In fact, she had a sub-manager below her on whom she depended to do "Issan things" with her Issanese (is that a word?) employees, such as reprimanding them in their native Isan language. But she and I were from basically the same place, so she at least promised to keep an eye out for me. A boss is a boss, and I knew that everything is about work and money, but it was still good to hear kind words from a mother-like figure.

As we were chatting and the seamstress was preparing that day's uniform for me, I saw that 7 P.M. was approaching. My boss's boss-body-clock must have been telling her the same thing, because she made a hand gesture outside the shophouse and summoned over a motorcycle taxi driver, who would take me and one of my new outfits back to the bar. She offered for me to change in the shophouse before going over to work, but I was too embarrassed to be seen in that outfit on the back of a motorcycle, so I chose to change in the bar instead. Once I became more familiar with bar work, I saw girls in even much more revealing outfits riding on motorcycles—but I myself never became any more willing to wear that outfit anywhere outside the bar.

When I reached the bar, I saw that several girls were already preparing for work. A few of them had the standard bargirl costume, a bikini that could easily be removed for topless dancing. But one of them had a costume that looked like mine, so I deduced she was also one of the "coyote" girls. She approached me before I approached her, introduced herself as Om, welcomed me to the bar, and said that the boss mentioned that a new girl (me) would be joining as a coyote dancer that day.

My first reaction upon meeting Om was not the camaraderie of meeting a coworker, but the panic of possibly having been found out. Om looked like many of my high school classmates and was about my age, and as I already mentioned, her being a coyote girl meant that she was probably from Bangkok. Had my bar life suddenly intersected with my home life? Fortunately not. Om soon mentioned that she was from Samut Prakan, the same town (near Bangkok) as the boss. As I later found out, Om's story was quite similar to mine, although with worse luck than mine, because she did previously have to work in the Ratchada brothels to pay off a "mafia bank" (loan shark) debt. Like me, Om didn't have a steady boyfriend, so it was understood, even though unsaid, between us that we were looking for foreign husbands on Soi Cowboy.

Meat Market

Suiting up for dancing on the stage, being asked my name and origins and life story by fellow coyote girls, hearing the loud American rock music playing in the bar, even smelling the stale cigarettes—it reinforced to me that I was now a *bargirl*. No way around it. I was a coyote girl, yes, and I was white-skinned, and all that, but until I was actually in the place, I hadn't really realized how very *bargirl* this life would be. Even if I thought I was better than or different from the job and its usual bargirls, here I was, working right alongside them, doing exactly the same thing. A part of me clung to toe Thai-style covering fiction of "I'm a coyote girl, not a bargirl," just as the bargirls clung to the fiction of "I'm a bargirl, not a prostitute," and maybe the street prostitutes clung to the fiction of "I'm a prostitute, not a whore." But the other part of me knew throughout my being that I was now entirely a bargirl, and this was the best that life could give me at that point, so all I could do was make the best of it.

"I'm only here to look for a stable foreign husband" was the comforting thought I started to run through my mind. But then, that's exactly why all the other girls were here. That's why even the bargirliest of the bargirls were here too. So it didn't separate me from my coworkers there. But it did remind me to focus on the customers, and what I could gain, rather than on my own temporary discomforts. "Keep your eye on the ball," as Americans say.

It wasn't difficult to focus on customers. They were all around me. All of them wanted to drink a beer and watch Thai girls dance. Of course. Which ones were willing to go farther than that? And I don't mean a night of sex back at the hotel. I mean, of course, a real, long-term relationship, or at the very least, a "daddy" relationship, like the one I was still cultivating with Aek, though in fear of him finding out where I worked now and recoiling in disgust.

I found dancing on the stage physically tiring. That sounds ridiculous, I know, when compared with the maids and factory workers and street sweepers in Thailand. I know. Still, my usual work that I was used to was just sitting and chatting and having a few drinks at the hostess club, or lounging around and giving a lazy one-hand handjob at the kapoo shop. Actually dancing on stage, or making some semblance of dancing (I don't think what we did was Olympics-level dancing!) was physically so stressful.

We were to work from 8 P.M. to 1 A.M., in two alternating shifts, so I could expect to be dancing about one third of the time, after accounting for break times and pauses and things like that. I know that anyone who's worked in a factory will laugh at me, but my legs and thighs and even shoulders were sore just one hour into the night. I was thinking – these experienced bargirls do this dancing and then go have sex with their customer all night! As much as foreigners sometimes pity bargirls for having sex for money, I think there's not enough appreciation for just the physical demands of the job, sex or not!

While trying to hide my grimace from muscle pain, I scanned the eyes of customers over and over. I knew one rule that everyone talks about in hostess bars, kapoo, massage, everywhere: Asian customers, usually from Japan and Singapore, are good as customers, and occasionally as sugar daddies, but will never marry or have a long-term relationship with a bargirl. They're probably more generous with money than Westerners when it's just a one-night sex transaction, or tips in the bar, but they can't be expected to truly fall in love on Soi Cowboy, or a hostess club, or a kapoo shop. In fact, they're just like Thai men in that way. I didn't want to repeat the unfulfilled expectations and needs of my relationship with Aek, so I stayed away from the Asian customers in the bar. If I wanted quick spending cash and tips, they would've been great, but I had to remind myself to focus on the long-term, and the potential of marriage.

Sometimes I did take advantage of the Japanese customers, in a way that I thought was hilarious, because of my past experience in Harajuku Girls, where I was a "Japanese girl" who didn't speak Thai and therefore pretended that I couldn't converse with the Thai customers. With the Japanese customers at Soi Cowboy, I didn't have to pretend, because I really was (and still am) a Thai girl, and really did not (and do not) speak Japanese. So it provided me with a shield of "sorry, I don't know what you're saying, so we have to keep this relationship down to you giving me a tip and watching me dance." A few of my more experienced coyote coworkers offered to help me learn key Japanese phrases, but I wasn't too interested in that. In fact, my key advantage over them was that I spoke pretty good English, unlike them, and I knew that if I found the right English-speaking foreigner, I could outdo them at least in communication ability, if not looks. Sure, I thought I was the prettiest girl there. Was I? Who knows. Maybe not for Westerners' tastes anyway. That's all debatable. But what's not debatable is my English was way better than theirs, and that's what mattered.

Bargirls are renowned for their English-language conversational abilities. No, actually, they're not. I know how Western tourists imitate bargirls. "Hello whatchoo name? You come flom? You buy me dlink?" First, I wasn't from Issan, so I could pronounce the letter r! You might not know, but saying l for r is only an Issan thing, because their dialect doesn't have an r sound. We Bangkok people pride ourselves on correctly pronouncing r. And other than being able to pronounce the letter r, I wasn't a professor of English literature, but I had at least finished mathayom (high school), and had watched enough undubbed American movies on DVDs and online so that I had no trouble making somewhat interesting English conversation. In fact, having worked at the hostess club taught me how to make interesting but nonthreatening conversation with men out for a night of fun – and it takes more than "where you come from?" Now all I had to do was translate those abilities to English, and the world of Western men, not more Aeks.

I definitely didn't want another Aek. I was still meeting the original Aek a few times a month for hotel sex dates, and that was all my time allowed, and also almost all that my short-term money needs demanded.

I was actually learning much less than the full-on bargirls. I collected only a basic salary, plus tips directly given to me (which the manager always attempted to have me "share" with her), plus commissions on drinks. If you have heard that Soi Cowboy bars cheat customers on the number of drinks charged, they also cheat us bargirls, although of course in the other direction, not giving us commissions for all the drinks we had bought, while charging customers for extra drinks that were never bought. Regular bargirls were collecting good money from sex fees. They would get around 500 baht ($15 USD) from the bar and about 2,000 baht ($65 USD) from the customer for every time they went to have sex with a customer. The more popular girls could do that several times a night, making a total income of a few hundred dollars a day – making in a day an amount that's normally a good monthly salary at that time (and even now) in Bangkok.

They were skilled at it. People often claim that Thai people are too relaxed about time, but my bargirl coworkers calculated their time down to the second. They even knew how long a taxi takes to various Bangkok hotels where their customers might be staying, so they charged higher prices to customers whose hotels required more travel time. And once they were back from the "excursion" with the customer, they'd brag to their coworkers about how quickly they were in and out (ha ha). The gold standard was one hour, including round-trip travel time. It would usually require going to one of the small rooms around Soi Cowboy, not a full hotel, but I saw some girls brag about making the one-hour gold standard even with taxi travel to a hotel.

That was the younger, more popular girls anyway. They were closer to my age, so in most ways I compared myself to them. But their goals were different from mine, as they were more interested in their current income, rather than in looking for a husband. The older girls, 30+, were more intensely looking for a husband, and would take their time with any man who presented the chance of being a husband or even boyfriend or sponsor. One girl was already over 40 – but looked good, very good, for her age – and she would sometimes go with customers free of charge in order to make them feel special when she thought one of them had long-term potential. Of course it was all a skilled game, and she went with them for "free" in the present because she hoped to get much more than 2,000 baht from them in long-term financial support. And it was a game that I watched and learned from, although didn't wholly adopt as my own. I preferred to adapt it to my style and my personality, and also to my goals. I wasn't interested in one-night stands for money, especially since I still had Aek – he usually initiated contact, but I knew that if I was hard up for cash, I could always initiate contact for a hotel sex date, and the next morning find about 5,000 baht he'd placed in my purse while I was showering. So when I interacted with Soi Cowboy customers, I had to set myself apart, and make myself seem worthy of marriage, not just a paid one-night stand. I had to be distinct and valuable, but not aloof or completely unapproachable. So I had to become bargirl, but not too bargirl.

I watched how the bargirls interacted with customers. It was diametrically different from how I'd ever interacted with Thai customers at the hostess club. A Soi Cowboy bargirl might approach a customer by slapping his arm or grabbing his crotch. At the hostess club, that would've had us instantly fired, and probably beaten up by the boss! Sure, foreigners were a lot less formal in their expectations of us. Well, they loved to "wai" us, but they didn't even realize that "wai" is a formal and antiquated gesture, and if anyone would be wai-ing anyone in Thai society, it would be the serving staff wai-ing the customer, not the other way around. But I saw that what foreigners accepted as playful or flirtatious were gestures that Thai customers at the hostess club, or even at the handjob shop, would've seen as unbelievably rude, probably so rude they'd never come back to that establishment again.

Still, I didn't want to become completely bargirl, and I didn't want to be one of those girls walking into the bar and slapping a foreigner man in the face and grabbing his crotch and showing him her nipple. We coyote girls were supposed to be more demure anyway, known in Thai as "reap roy" ("proper female politeness"). It was useful to adopt some of what I saw in the bar from their interactions, but I also didn't want to become completely like them. First, it just wasn't my style, my way of being. But secondly, I wanted to stand out and be something and someone different from the usual bargirl experience foreigners would have.

So if I saw a customer looking and smiling at me when I was dancing, when my fifteen-minute dancing shift was over, I'd go over and shock him with my English. It was usually safe to comment on the shirt he was wearing or on his model of phone. My English was good enough and my questions well-formed enough that it shocked the men who were used to coming to bars in Thailand, as they'd certainly never expected that. No, my English wasn't and isn't perfect, even now. But compared to the broken pidgin English my coworkers (meaning, Thai bar girls in general) spoke? My English was spectacular!

And the men who were "fresh from the airport," as we said, the ones who had just arrived in Thailand and hadn't had much experience in the bars, they didn't even know to be surprised. They just assumed that we'd all be speaking fluent English. In fact, that's how I was able to distinguish the repeat sex tourists from the fresh-off-the-airplane customers. If a customer was flabbergasted (that's a great English word!) by my English ability, I knew that he'd been around the Bangkok bars for at least a while. If he responded to my English queries without surprise, I knew that he was fresh to the bargirl scene.

Well, what difference did it make? Please let me ask you: if you are a man looking for a Thai girlfriend, do you want one who has had just a few boyfriends, or one who has hundreds of boyfriends on call? Well for us girls, even if not bargirls, any man who has been hanging around the Thai bar scene is a man who has hundreds of girls "on call," sometimes literally on call, stored in his phone directory. That's fine for him. That's what going to prostitutes is for. But that means he's much less likely to settle down as a husband for just one special girl. So if a girl wants to be that one special girl for a lifetime, she knows to skip over a man who has a lot of experience and contacts among Thai bargirls. If she just wants to get paid for a night of sex, then it doesn't matter. If she just wants a short-term boyfriend or sponsor, then it matters only a little bit: a man who plays around with many bargirls might still be good for some gifts and dinners, but you're always competing with all the others in his phone directory, past present and future. But if a man is fresh to the bargirl scene, it is more likely that your only competition for his affection will be a few women, maybe friends and ex-girlfriends, most likely back in his home country—those are odds I could live with! And when I imagined "the competition" for the affection of the ideal foreign husband I'd hoped to meet, I imagined a man who hadn't spent a lot of time with bargirls, and my competition as far as bargirls would be just the girls immediately around me who might want to attract his immediate attention—but once I had his attention in his bar, I would have to compete only with his few girlfriends or lovers or ex-girlfriends in his real life, and not with hundreds or thousands of topless Issan girls fawning over him.

Some nights I flirted with all the customers, hoping to get tips and bought commission-drinks. It was an acceptable way to make money, similar to work in the hostess club, but more physically demanding—although after the first week or so, I felt my body much stronger than before, and the dancing wasn't a big problem, and even Aek commented that I had more muscles than before. But other nights, I just wasn't in much of a mood to beg for tips and drinks. I focused on any guys who could be long-term relationship (husband) material for me, and was pretty aloof to the other customers. That's ok. As coyote dancers, we were not like the hostesses in the hostess bar. Chatting with customers was not our primary duty. In fact, most of my fellow coyote dancers didn't speak any English, so chatting with customers couldn't be their primary duty. So on those not-feeling-it nights, I really only did my minimum, dancing on stage, accepting tips when offered, and keeping an eye out for top-class, prime "husband targets." If a man didn't fit that category, I didn't pay much attention to him.

My eyes were good for finding husband targets, but no better than other girls'. Remember I was in a bar with about five other coyote dancers and about thirty regular bargirls. Most of them would be very interested in a foreign husband, even those who had Thai husbands and children. So I couldn't count on beating them to the target, and I couldn't really count on finding a target they couldn't see. We were all in the same bar, seeing the same selection of men. And they had a lot more experience with foreigners than I did, so they were probably better readers of foreigners too. I had no chance of beating them at initially spotting our, uhh, prey. My advantage would come at the presumable screening stage: my English, my comparative ability to make meaningful conversation, my English, my lack of kids and past husbands, and, of course, my English.

Were they really prey? I didn't think so then and I still don't think so now. I may have hated some or many of the customers in the bar (unbeknownst to them), but I never hated my imagined husband I'd meet in the bar. He was, at least in my imagination, free of the faults of the other bar customers: the bad breath, the miserly low tips, the milk-and-cheese smells, the sexually transmitted diseases, the yellow socks, the deftly concealed wives and children.

What kind of man was I looking for? If any bargirl is asked that question, she'll describe her ideal man as "take care me." I don't know whether I should be ashamed that this was also my main criterion. I did want a man to provide me and my family with a long-term financial future. Without it, my future, and any non-rich Thai person's future, would be bleak. Most low-level jobs in Thailand, such as being a store clerk, are not open to people over thirty years old. Without education or skills beyond mathayom (high school), I was only qualified for that level job, and 30 wasn't that far away. Many jobs are even only open to people of a certain skin shade – employment ads will say that you have to be light skinned or at least not too dark skinned – fortunately my skin is sufficiently fair to qualify for anything, but that's only a matter of luck. And while there are some minimal government programs in Thailand to help the poor, they are really almost nothing, and they are usually only available to people who are politically connected to their local government officials. There's nothing like social security or government pensions for old or sick people in Thailand. Maybe the closest thing would be going to the nearest temple and asking for help, but temples don't provide anything to the poor more than a sleeping mat and a (small) bowl of rice.

Thai men could, if they were not born into wealth, hope to become policemen or soldiers, become players in the Thai game of corruption and dirty dealings, and secure themselves financial futures. Some of the few real rags-to-riches stories in Thailand are of working-class boys who became policemen and rose up to become US dollar multimillionaires. I know in America a policeman is considered a usually respected figure, but not a particularly powerful or rich job. Thai people look upon a policeman as someone who's made it financially. We don't respect them much as moral figures, but we see them as successful players in the Thai game. The story is similar for soldiers. The Thai army doesn't go to war, but they are involved in coups and do a lot of dirty business and have big government budgets. Becoming a soldier and rising up through the ranks is a good way for a boy from a modest background to become financially secure or maybe even rich. The top soldiers in Thailand make a lot more money than the top businessmen, which I know must be shocking if you come from a first-world country. But then, in Thailand, the army and the police are big businesses.

Are any of these routes available to women? No. It's unthinkable for a Thai woman to rise to a high-level, lucrative position in the Thai police or military organizations. There are female soldiers and police officers, but they are never in the positions of authority where they get to handle budgets and collect bribes. They are usually given the jobs that aren't lucrative enough for the men, the jobs that have no connection to the big money. Of course, in the Thai military and police, as in the hostess clubs and everywhere else in Thailand, many or most of the women are there in hopes of mingling with rich men who will marry or support them. There's no independent path to financial security in Thailand, other than by latching on to a man who has that kind of security.

My every step when dancing on the stage was full of all these thoughts and ideas and common knowledge, things that are common knowledge to any Thai, especially a woman, but maybe not to you, and not to the customers in the bar. The usual Westerner's vision of a prostitute's or stripper's (I guess the Western equivalent of a coyote dancer) life goes like: girl is born, encounters difficult situation like a debt or a drug problem, starts doing something desperate for cash, and here I am, the Western white knight who's saving her. In my case, sure, I had the fire in my family's restaurant, but something like a fire is just a normal fact of life, and just part of being working-class or poor in Thailand. I wasn't from an especially hard background. Some of my coworkers were in fact from personal and family histories of many tragedies, but some weren't. It wasn't specific or tragedies or specific life events that had set us selling our bodies and souls on a stage. It was just the fact of being born not rich and not even male in Thailand, a place that is completely set up as a game for the rich, and especially for rich men.

So it shouldn't surprise you that we seek to latch on to rich men. Better yet, to rich foreign men, who don't have the belief that the system of "the rich men own everything" is the natural order, even if we ourselves actually kind of believe it is indeed the natural order.

I ended up giving my phone number and email address to about one man a week. This was before Facebook was popular in Thailand, although we did have a social network called hi5, which I was surprised to learn no Western man had ever heard of! I was also hesitantly trying my luck on a dating website, ThaiLoveLinks, although most of the men I found on that website were living far away and just wanted some attention from a pretty girl, without having any plans or money to make a real relationship.

The men I met in the bar actually seemed more like marriage prospects than the ones I met in online dating, which even at the time I knew sounds ridiculous, but it's true. Maybe it was just because the men in the bars were already in Thailand, while most of the men online were only dreaming about visiting Thailand.

From the conversations I had with those men in the bars, some of which were actually hopeful and not bad conversations, I was having hope I could actually find one to love me. None of them were perfect. Of course some or most were very interested in "come to the hotel room" rather than discussing a future together. But it would be the same for meeting men to date in any setting, probably anywhere in the world, so how can I complain?

Through those contacts, one shone through. I had met him in my second month of working on Soi Cowboy. His name — Rich — still requires explanation to my Thai friends and relatives who aren't familiar with English names. Well, maybe I would've had more explaining to Thai people to do if my fiancé's name had been Dick, although fewer Thai people know the word "dick" than know "rich."

Unlike the case with Aek, I didn't notice Rich in any extraordinary way when he entered the bar. No, he didn't sweep me off my feet, and no, it wasn't love at first sight. Those are Western concepts anyway. As I told you, Thai love is more practical than that.

He was just an average Western guy, about forty years old, with a big nose and blue eyes, coming in alone and sitting down, dressed as though he'd just finished a business meeting. I didn't pay much attention. I started paying attention to him only when I saw how much he'd enjoyed watching me dance, staring at me with a smile of enjoyment and appreciation, rather than the usual leering smile of a pervert imagining me dancing on his cock back in his hotel room.

My fifteen-minute dancing shift was almost over when he first came in to the bar and started looking at me. When I finished, I ascertained he was excited enough to make him ready for an approach. I was grateful my shift didn't go longer than that, because he might have lost interest or excitement or moved on to another girl if he'd had to wait longer. I got off the stage and approached him with a pickup line I'd just devised.

My brilliant pickup line: "Your collar is unbuttoned." It worked. He laughed as if I'd just told him the funniest joke in the world. Which of course I had. I took him off guard. He had been going around Soi Cowboy just a few days during his business trip, but had already learned the "whatchoo name, you come flom?" routine. So my query in my reasonably good English, had thrown him off.

As I already mentioned, my greatest assets were not T&A (Tits & Ass) but E&C (English and Conversation). I was (and still am!) a pretty good-looking girl by Thai standards, but as far as I know and as far as I could see in the bar, the Westerners didn't really subscribe to those beauty standards. It's my English and my pickup line that at first attracted him, and ultimately served to change my life.

His shirt collar was in fact unbuttoned. He had been a little bit too eager in taking off his tie in his hotel room before proceeding down to Soi Cowboy. That served as a natural entry point into a natural conversation. I had only been in the bar scene a few months, so I wasn't accustomed to the "you hansom, you buy me dlink" routine, the routine that he told me had been a huge turnoff when he visited other bars. It was the routine I was consciously trying to avoid falling into, although I did have a latent fear that given enough time in the bar scene, I'd lose my different-ness and become too much like the other girls. With Richard, keeping in mind that the bargirl ethos was a turnoff, I did my best, in fact, to act like the twentysomething girls I'd seen on Friends and other American TV shows, and as little as possible like a bargirl. I'm not sure whether he also did his best to act like a twentysomething guy from Friends and as little as possible like a sex tourist! Maybe.

At least he wasn't a sex tourist. Mostly not, anyway. It was his first time in Thailand. He worked as a sales engineer for an American construction-related company, the kind of company that builds huge bridges and skyscrapers. As I later found out, the reason he'd looked at me and smiled that much in the bar was that he'd just had a breakup with a Taiwanese-American girlfriend who apparently looked and even moved and talked a lot like me, and when he saw me on stage, it elicited his best memories of her. While he was in Thailand on a business trip, he did admit that he missed "Asian sex" (whatever that means!) with his ex girlfriend and that he was hoping to get some "Asian sex" while he was visiting.

Fair enough, as Americans say. All the men I'd meet in the bar were looking for sex. And he was just a guy shaken up after a breakup and looking for comfort sex, not a chronic sex tourist. It did strike me as funny that for once, a Western man would appreciate me for my fair-skinned looks, although seemingly more because I reminded him of his fair-skinned Asian ex-girlfriend, and not really because he preferred fair-skinned girls overall.

My fifteen-minute chat with him made me tremendously comfortable with him. I had never asked him about his marital or relationship status, and during that initial chat, he hadn't yet told me about his ex-girlfriend whom I apparently physically resembled. In fact, with the loud music playing in the bar and the bargirls dancing in front of our faces, and with my good but still not perfect English, a fifteen-minute bar chat had about as much useful information as a thirty-second normal chat. We didn't get much across, other than him complimenting my natural manner and my English. But I just felt good about the whole thing, and I even had inclinations that this might become a long-term thing – ridiculous after a fifteen-minute chat, but we Thai people do believe in something like "love at first sight," although in the Thai explanation, it's more like "destined to be together and recognize each other suddenly." I believe in that stuff much less than most Thai people do, and normally I just laugh at it, but this time, I felt something a lot like that.

I didn't want to be too forward or aggressive or slutty (here I was, dancing on stage in a bikini, concerned about being seen as slutty...), nor to seem too desperate, so I didn't ask him for any contact information when I knew my fifteen minutes were going to be over. I just asked him if he'd be staying in the bar another fifteen minutes, so I could come back to him after I finished dancing. The answer was yes. It was just a small thing, but I interpreted that "yes" as meaning so much, almost meaning a commitment. I know it sounds silly. But it turned out to be true, so can you really say it's so silly?

In our second fifteen-minute chat, he seemed to be picking up that I liked him. He hadn't yet been spoiled by Thai bargirls throwing themselves at every Western man, so he didn't just assume that I'd automatically be throwing myself at him. So he was cautious in his approach, not wanting to overstep, acting as he would've acted meeting a woman in a Starbucks back in California, and similarly to how I didn't start with "you buy me dlink," he didn't start with "here's two thousand baht and I'm gonna fuck you good."

I hadn't actually picked up on his name. During the first fifteen minutes, he said his name was Rich, and I heard correctly, but thought

I heard wrong and it was just my funny fantasies playing a trick on my ears, and that he'd had something else but I'd just heard it as "rich" and maybe the next guy's name would sound like "handsome." So this time he repeated his name, then wrote it out on his iphone to make sure I could understand. He didn't even think that his name would be funny for Thai people, perhaps because Americans aren't as focused on the common noun "rich" as we Thais are.

I wanted to meet him again, more so than had been the case with any of the other customers I'd met in the bar. With them, I had some hesitation and some apprehensions from the beginning, but with Rich, it always felt right. That's not the same thing as saying he's perfect. Nobody is perfect, especially not me. But even though I could see that he had a few gray hairs and wasn't perfectly slim and was only middle-class and not really a rich Rich, but it all felt right, maybe even more right than it would've felt with a too-perfect guy.

I didn't want to "meet after the bar closes tonight," not only because I didn't want too seem to desperate, but because I didn't want to fit into the usual pattern of bargirl sex. At that point I'd had sex with only two previous customers from the bar – remember we coyote girls officially "didn't go home with customers" ("yeah, we only went to their hotel rooms!" as one of my coworkers liked to point out) – and I still wanted to completely separate this time with Rich from those other times. I told him we can meet the following evening around 7 P.M. and I'd take the day off from work. I reserved the whole evening for him. I gave him my phone number and he awkwardly gave me a business card to his hotel and hand-wrote his room number and full name on it. He didn't even have a Thai sim card in his phone, which was also a good sign.

We did meet that night, awkwardly, in the lobby of his hotel. As soon as I entered the lobby and spotted him waiting for me, I ran out of there with him like a scalded animal, so terrified was I of him seeing me as a girl who comes to his hotel room and immediately goes upstairs for sex. He took me to a sushi restaurant he'd discovered at a nearby mall, Emporium.

Did I tell him that Aek and I had often eaten there? No. When he asked me whether I have a boyfriend, what did I reply? No. Was I lying? No. I had always lamented to myself that Aek isn't really my boyfriend. Now that previously unpleasant thought was a source of freedom and happiness – freedom to find something better, and to hope for a future with Rich.

We did have sex that night. After walking around Emporium, he asked me whether I want to come back to his hotel room. He saw me dancing on a stage on Soi Cowboy; I couldn't pretend not to know what that means, or pretend not to know what sex is. I said yes, and only hoped that he wouldn't try to pay me for the sex. The most awkward part was telling him to stop at a pharmacy on our way back to the hotel room and buy condoms. I hoped he wouldn't say that he has a few in his wallet, and pleasantly enough, he only giggled like a teenage boy and pointed to a pharmacy across the street, and did not knowingly whip a twelve-pack of condoms out of his wallet.

The sex was incredible. I remember him on top of me multiple times and me tugging on his balls begging him to come because I couldn't stand any more orgasms. It was the truth and he knew it. It wasn't a huge penis (in fact, it was just regular sized) or a hot body (again, just average) that made me so aroused and sexually satisfied. It was that when I felt his arms around me, I felt something real, more real than I'd felt ever, since maybe my high school boyfriend. It was much more real than anything with Aek, or even with any of the other hand-picked customers from the hostess club and the bar with whom I'd hand-pickedly had sex.

It was a new world opening to me. Sex that would be fulfilling. A man loving me. He told me that he loves me when we showered together. Thai people normally don't say it, especially not in English, so

I only smiled and kissed his nose, and was smiling and almost crying from the emotion.

Before I was too into him, I asked him repeatedly about whether he has a wife back home, and he told me in great detail the story of his ex-girlfriend. It was so usual and normal that I almost wish he'd told me less detail, because it was boring stuff. They'd had the normal couple fights, until she finally left him and started dating her boss. Thank you, Lin (her name) for giving me Rich. You saved my life.

Exit Strategy

Did Rich really save my life? In some sense, yes. I wouldn't have died on the spot had I not met him that evening. I likely would have found some other man and had some other life with him. But I can't imagine any happier situation than the one I've found with Rich. Because he doesn't treat me as "just a bargirl," he took it as a matter of course that I'd continue my education in America, and I'm attending community college now and working on my writing skills. Community college isn't Harvard (where Thai people love to go), but it's a good start. We are married and living a nice low-key, low-profile life. We send money to my parents to help them out, and they are tremendously grateful and only "complain" that the $1,000 per month we send is too generous.

Maybe I saved Rich's life too. After his recent breakup, he could've become one of the many casualties of Thai bargirls, the more famous stories you always read about. He could've been extorted for $10,000 a month or been thrown out of a skyscraper or some such thing! Well, this makes me feel ridiculous too, because it's as if I'm saying I'm such a great girlfriend and wife because I didn't throw my husband off a skyscraper. But maybe among Thai bargirls that's a thing.

I never talked to Aek again, and he never contacted me either. Maybe he asked around about me and found out I'd moved to America, or maybe he found a younger or fairer-skinned upgrade. It doesn't matter to me, and of course I wish him happiness.

My coworkers at the bar, especially the coyote girls, are now quite attached to the idea of learning conversational English. Usually English schools near Bangkok's bar areas market their services to frustrated Western boyfriends (basic English classes advertised in English!) who want their girlfriends to be able to understand them. The "students" half-heartedly attend the classes, always held in the late afternoon to fit bargirl hours, to please their boyfriends. But my coworkers got the sudden idea that they would find instant white husband paradise if they learned good conversational English beyond "buy me dlink." They firmly believed that it's the only thing that brought me such a good outcome. Actually, they didn't know or care about how happy I am, but for them, any marriage to a foreign man is a good outcome, and they saw me get it.

The fiancee visa and the actual logistical process wasn't actually difficult. We Thai people somehow are taught that leaving Thailand is the most difficult thing in the world. I didn't find it difficult, and I didn't even find settling down in America difficult, other than learning to drive a car on the "wrong" side of the road, and sometimes having to repeat myself with my accented English to make myself understood. I drop by the Thai temple in our city sometimes, but it's dominated by ex-bargirls and seems to be a rehashing of the bargirl culture of gambling and hunting for an upgrade white man (in fact, on my first visit they told me that now that I'm in the US, I should start hunting for a richer man), so I stay away from them.

I wish I could tell you hilarious or embarrassing stories about cultural misunderstandings in my life in America, but there aren't any. I had lived in Bangkok long enough and watched enough American movies so nothing was shocking or baffling. I was never – here's that word again – flabbergasted. I didn't ask Rich's parents where they keep their water buffaloes, I didn't try to bribe any policemen, and I didn't start doing a bargirl dance in the middle of step-aerobics class.

Maybe the closest thing to "culture shock" is really more about the difference between a city center (Bangkok, where I grew up) and the suburbs (where I now live with Rich). I don't miss my old job in Bangkok, although I do miss the constant hum and flashing lights of a busy city — suburban America is a different quiet. Well, I want to be a mom soon, and I definitely think the American kind of quiet is a better atmosphere for raising kids. And the farther I can get away from the anxious thumping of dance music and the yelling sexual come-ons of the customers, the better. Even if in suburban America, I can't get a plate of pad thai at 3 AM. Having to cook my pad thai myself is worth this calmer, saner lifestyle. And Rich swears that he adores my cooking.

The practicalities of moving to America weren't amazing, but my story overall is I think an amazing one, and that's why I wanted to tell it. I lived something like the typical atypical bargirl life. From handjobs for ash to hostessing to finding the love of my life – yes, in a bar. You've seen my innermost thoughts, and the inside story of Thai society, and a Thai young woman's life. That's a Thai girl completely revealed, naked.

Afterword: Dispelling the Myths

There are many myths generally believed by foreigners. They are all false, but foreigners really cling to them, often because their Thai girlfriends insist they are true! But they're not really true. Here are the important ones I want to dispel:

- **Myth 1:** Thai girls prefer to be with foreign men. The most desirable Thai girls date or marry foreigners.

- **Myth 2:** Thai girls prefer older men. Age differences don't matter in Thailand.

- **Myth 3:** Prostitution is legal in Thailand. Being a prostitute is just a regular job in Thai society.

- **Myth 4:** Thai people always stick together, especially against foreigners. Thai people can count on one another to help in times of need.

- **Myth 5:** Some prostitution venues have higher class girls, university students from high society backgrounds.

Let me break these down for you, one by one, with the kind of naked honesty I promised you at the start of this book.

Myth 1: The "Preference" for Foreign Men

YOU WALK DOWN THE STREET in Bangkok and see a beautiful Thai woman on the arm of a foreigner. You think, "Wow, Thai girls really love Western guys!" You might even think we love your blue eyes, your big noses, or your "romantic" hearts.

I hate to break it to you, but usually, Thai girls don't date foreigners because they *prefer* them over Thai men. They date foreigners because Thai men don't want them.

In Thailand, the beauty standard is very strict: you have to be pale, white-skinned, and look like a Korean pop star. If you have dark skin—which is common for girls from the Isaan region where most bargirls come from—Thai men will call you *e-dam* ("blackie") and look down on you. They see dark skin as a sign of being a poor farmer.

So, here is the situation: A girl is rejected by Thai men because of her skin color or her age (if she is over 25). Then she meets a foreigner who tells her she is "exotic" and beautiful exactly because of that dark skin. Of course she goes with the foreigner! It isn't a cultural preference for Western men; it is an economic and social necessity. As I mentioned earlier about my own search for a husband, we are practical people. If the local market rejects you, you look to the export market.

Myth 2: The Ageless Lover

THIS IS THE FAVORITE myth of every 60-year-old man who comes to Thailand and finds a 20-year-old girlfriend. He tells his friends back home, "In Thailand, age is just a number. They respect elders."

Age is not just a number in Thailand. It is a very big number. We young Thai girls are not genuinely sexually attracted to grandfathers. We like cool, handsome young guys just as much as women in your country do.

But remember, we are looking for survival. An older man represents stability. He is what we call a "Daddy" in the truest sense—a provider. In fact, many girls in the industry actually prefer much older men, not for romance, but for logistics. An older man is less likely to cheat, he is more likely to stay home, and—I will be brutal here—he is more likely to die sooner.

It sounds cold, but for a girl from a poor village, marrying an older foreigner is like signing a caregiving contract. She takes care of his body and health, and in exchange, he secures her financial future and hopefully leaves her a house or pension when he is gone. It is a trade: her youth for his security.

Myth 3: The Myth of Legality

BECAUSE YOU SEE MASSAGE parlors, karaoke bars, and red-light districts like Soi Cowboy everywhere, you assume prostitution must be legal. Or at least, that the police are protecting the girls.

Actually, prostitution is strictly illegal. The laws are very clear. The reason it exists everywhere is not because the law allows it, but because of what we call "tea money."

Every bar, every massage shop, and every karaoke joint pays a monthly bribe to the local police station. The police are not there to enforce the law; they are the "silent partners" in the business. As I told you about my own work, we live in the gray areas. When you hear about a "raid" on the news, it is usually because someone didn't pay their tea money, or because the police need to put on a show for the politicians.

This makes life very dangerous for the girls. Because our job is technically illegal, we have no labor rights. If a boss cheats us or a customer hurts us, we can't easily go to the police, because we are criminals in the eyes of the law. The visibility of the sex trade is just proof of how deep the corruption goes.

Myth 4: The Myth of Thai Unity

FOREIGNERS LOVE TO talk about the "Village Culture" of Thailand. You think we are all one big happy family who help each other. You see us smiling and assume we are kind to everyone.

But there is a difference between *Nam Jai* (water of the heart, or genuine kindness) and *Kreng Jai* (fear of causing trouble or losing face). Most of what you see is *Kreng Jai*. We smile because we don't want confrontation.

In reality, Thai society is very loose. We take care of our own family and our own boss (our patron), but we often ignore strangers. It is like having "tunnel vision." If there is a car accident on the road, many Thais will just drive by or stand and watch without helping. We believe in Karma—if someone is having bad luck, maybe it is their own karma, and we don't want to get involved and bring bad luck to ourselves.

As I told you about my family's restaurant fire—neighbors didn't come rushing to give us money. We were on our own. The idea that all Thais stick together is a nice fairy tale they teach us in school, but in the real world of Bangkok, it is every family for itself.

Myth 5: The "Good Girl" Student

THIS IS THE MARKETING trick that makes men spend the most money. You will see ads for "Sideline" girls, or girls in "Gentlemen's Clubs" who claim to be university students, models, or "High Society" (*Hiso*) girls doing this for pocket money.

It is a fantasy. I worked in a place that pretended we were Japanese, remember? It is the same thing. Calling a girl a "Sideline" or a "Student" is just a way to charge 5,000 or 10,000 baht instead of 2,000 baht.

Real High Society girls in Thailand are incredibly protective of their "face" and reputation. Their families have millions. They would never risk being seen in the sex trade for a few thousand baht. It would destroy their family name.

While there are students who do sex work to pay for tuition or luxury bags, they are girls from desperately poor backgrounds trying to survive or fit in, not boredom-stricken rich kids. The "Sideline" label allows the customer to pretend he isn't with a prostitute, and it allows the girl to pretend she isn't one. It helps everyone maintain the illusion, but at the end of the day, it is still just a transaction.

Also by Noi Thawattana

We're Not Supposed to Tell You: Sex Slavery, Drugs, and Other
Secrets of Thailand's Prostitution Industry
Thai Girl Naked: A Former Bangkok Bargirl Tells All

www.ingramcontent.com/pod-product-compliance
Lightning Source LLC
Chambersburg PA
CBHW071100290526
45795CB00004B/1582